SPIRITUAL WARFARE
BUILDING YOUR BATTLE PLAN

PASTOR STEVEN PRATT, JR.

Copyright © 2026 by Canada Church Planting
All Scripture quotations are taken from the King James Version (KJV).

All rights reserved. No part of this book may be reproduced, stored in a retrieval system, or transmitted in any form or by any means, electronic, mechanical, photocopy, recording, or otherwise, without the written permission of the publisher, except for brief quotations in printed reviews.

To contact us or order:
email@canadachurchplanting.com
http://www.canadachurchplanting.com

Contents

Dedication	v
Acknowledgments	vii
Author's Note	ix
How to Use This Book	xi

PART 1: CHOOSE YOUR SIDE

Chapter 1: Before You Fight, You Must Belong	3
Battle Plan: Choose Your Side	15

PART 2: THE ATTACK

Chapter 2: Recognizing the Attack	21
Battle Plan: Recognize the Attack	45
Chapter 3: Responding to the Attack	53
Battle Plan: Respond to the Attack	65
Chapter 4: Preventing the Attack	77
Battle Plan: Prevent the Attack	87

PART 3: THE BATTLEFIELD

Chapter 5: The Battleground	95
Battle Plan: The Battleground	111
Chapter 6: The Weapons	117
Battle Plan: The Weapons	139
Chapter 7: The Armor	149
Battle Plan: The Armor	161

PART 4: THE STRATEGY OF VICTORY

Chapter 8: The Mindset of the Warrior	169
Battle Plan: The Mindset	185
Chapter 9: The Movement of the Spirit	191
Battle Plan: The Spirit	201
Chapter 10: The Mission of the Army	211
Battle Plan: The Mission	227

PART 5: THE FINAL BATTLE PLAN

Chapter 11: The Final Battle Plan	235
The Final Charge	242
About the Author	244

| *Dedication* |

To my Pastor and my friend...

Thank you, Pastor Josh, for standing with me and my family through some of the darkest spiritual attacks we've ever faced. You've been there when I needed it most. Your steady counsel, compassionate heart, and unwavering support have meant more than words can express.

This book is dedicated to you for the lessons you've taught me, the strength you've helped me find, and the example you've set as both a shepherd and a friend. I pray this book helps others the way you've helped me.

Acknowledgments

This book was not written alone. It was forged through battle, sustained by prayer, and shaped by the faithful people God placed in my life.

First and above all, I thank the *Lord Jesus Christ*, my Saviour, my strength, and the One who gives me every bit of truth I have. Without Him, I could claim no victory, and the fight itself would have no purpose.

To my wife, Laura: your steadfast love, your faith, and your quiet encouragement have anchored me through every season of ministry and every spiritual attack. You have stood beside me in the darkest moments. You are a gift from God, and I thank Him for you every single day.

To my children: I love you more than you know, and I pray for you every day. This book is part of the legacy I want to leave you, one that I hope teaches you to stand strong and fight faithfully in the power of the Lord.

Thank you to *Angie Vega* and *Ligaya Pinga* for your tireless help with editing, and to my church family at *FaithWay Bible Baptist Church* for walking with me in prayer and allowing me to shepherd you through your battles. Your faithfulness has shaped me more than you know.

And to *every believer* under spiritual attack: this book is for you. May God use it to equip His soldiers for the fight ahead.

| Author's Note |

You did not pick up this book by accident! If you are holding it in your hands or reading its pages, it is likely because you have felt something pressing against your spiritual life, something unseen yet very real. Perhaps it came in the form of discouragement, confusion, temptation, or fear.

Maybe you have struggled with overwhelming thoughts or an internal battle that defies explanation. You have asked questions like, *"What is wrong with me?"* or *"Why do I feel like I am being attacked?"* If so, you are not alone.

I have asked those same questions. I have wrestled through seasons of spiritual attack. I have seen it in my own life, and I have walked with many others through it as a pastor. The reality of spiritual warfare is not theoretical. It is a tangible and profound experience. And it is not limited to those in full-time ministry. Every believer, regardless of maturity or background, will face battles that extend beyond the physical and emotional. These are spiritual attacks, and they are on the rise.

Spiritual warfare is not a metaphor. It is a reality. There is an enemy of your soul, Satan, and the Bible makes it clear that he, along with his fallen angels, actively seeks to oppose the work of God in your life. He does not always strike with force.

More often, he works through subtle lies, quiet distractions, lingering doubts, or hidden compromises. But the damage is real. Unless you know how to recognize his attacks and respond biblically, you may find yourself worn down, discouraged, or even spiritually defeated.

This book exists to help you understand the battle you are in and prepare you to stand faithfully in it. It is intentionally structured in five parts, each one guiding you deeper into recognizing the enemy's work, strengthening your spiritual defenses, and learning how to stand firm in Christ. Together, these sections will help you build a *Personal Battle Plan* rooted in Scripture and lived out in daily obedience.

In the *Battle Plan* section of each chapter, you will begin shaping your plan step by step. You will record what God is showing you, identify where the enemy has worked, and write down practical steps you can take to prepare for the battle ahead. By the end of the book, these pieces will be brought together into a single, strategic *Personal Battle Plan* you can rely on when the pressure returns.

Because the battle does not end with one season. Satan is real and actively seeks to devour, distract, or divide. But you do not have to face him unprepared. Through Christ, you are not only equipped. *You are empowered!*

Victory does not come through self-discipline, motivational slogans, or emotional highs. It comes through the truth of God's Word and the power of His Spirit at work in you. If you belong to Christ, that power is already yours. So do not rush through these pages. Slow down. Pray. Reflect. Let the Lord speak to you as you build your spiritual defenses and prepare for the battles ahead.

In the fight with you,

Pastor Steven Pratt, Jr.

| *How to Use This Book* |

This is more than a book. It is a battle guide. If you feel spiritually under attack, whether mentally, emotionally, or even physically, you are not imagining it. The enemy is real, and this book is here to help you fight back with biblical truth.

Each chapter addresses a key aspect of spiritual warfare and exposes how the enemy operates. This book is not only about learning. It is about preparing for battle and engaging the fight.

As you read, you will be building your Personal Battle Plan, a strategy tailored to your life, rooted in Scripture, and designed to help you fight, resist, and stand firm when attacks come.

Here is how to use this book:

1. **Read one chapter at a time.** Each chapter builds on the last. Go slowly and allow God's Word to prepare you for the battles ahead.

2. **Complete the Battle Plan section.** At the end of each chapter, you will work on your Battle Plan by reflecting, responding, and taking action against the enemy's attacks.

3. **Assemble your final strategy.** At the end of the book, you will gather your responses into a complete Personal Battle Plan. This will become a spiritual weapon you can return to whenever new attacks come.

4. **Share it with others.** Use this book in personal devotions, small groups, or biblical counseling. Revisit it often, and help others learn how to fight well.

5. **Do not fight alone.** If you are struggling, speak with your pastor or a trusted spiritual ally. God never intended His people to wage war in isolation.

This war is real. But through Christ, you are not powerless. You are equipped for battle, and this book is designed to help you engage the fight faithfully.

By the time you finish, you will not just understand the war you are in. You will have a clear and personal battle plan you can follow when the enemy attacks again.

PART ONE

CHOOSE YOUR SIDE

*Before you fight the battle,
you must decide whom you serve.*

1

BEFORE YOU FIGHT, YOU MUST BELONG

Before you take your stand against the enemy,
you must first kneel before your King.

There are moments in life when something feels off, but you can't quite put your finger on it. It's more than stress, worse than just a bad day. It's a spiritual pressure, unseen but real. The Bible makes this clear: *"For we wrestle not against flesh and blood, but against principalities, against powers, against the rulers of the darkness of this world, against spiritual wickedness in high places"* (Ephesians 6:12). In other words, what you're feeling isn't only the weight of life. It's the weight of war.

You sense it when you try to pray and your mind keeps wandering, refusing to stay focused. You know it when thoughts intrude that you never invited in. You feel it when temptation presses harder than usual, when fear creeps in without warning, leaving you drained, discouraged, and distant from God.

And here's the troubling part. It doesn't always make sense. The attack isn't always dramatic or obvious. Sometimes it slips in quietly, through the loss of desire for prayer, through a coldness toward

Spiritual Warfare: Building Your Battle Plan

Scripture, through the slow erosion of your hunger for God. That's no accident. It's the mark of an enemy at work.

This book is written for those moments. Not for the days when life is easy, but for the nights when you're barely holding on. For the times when you've prayed, read your Bible, even sat in church faithfully, yet you still feel stuck, still under pressure, still sensing that something isn't right.

I remember a conversation with a faithful man in our church. He was always willing, always ready to serve. On the outside, nothing seemed wrong. But when we sat down to talk, his words revealed a deeper struggle. *"Pastor, I don't even know what's wrong with me. I wake up with anxiety for no reason. I lose my temper over little things. I feel far from God. I pray, but it's like a wall stands between me and the Lord."*

That man wasn't crazy. He wasn't weak. He wasn't beyond help. He was under attack. A spiritual war raged in his life, and he didn't know how to fight it.

Maybe that sounds familiar. Maybe that's exactly where you are. You've prayed, tried to read your Bible, shown up at church, and still the struggle continues. The harder you try, the heavier the pressure grows. That's not coincidence. That's warfare.

This isn't about blaming everything on the devil or excusing our own choices. We all carry responsibility before God. It's about understanding the reality behind the attack. There is an enemy, and unless you learn to recognize and resist him, you'll keep fighting the same battles again and again.

Before we go further, there's a question that must be answered. It's the most important question you'll ever face.

Do you belong to Christ?

You cannot fight a spiritual war if you are not spiritually alive.

You cannot overcome the enemy if you have never been born again. Without Christ, you walk into battle unarmed and unprotected.

Chapter 1: Before You Fight, You Must Belong

You have no spiritual weapon, no God-given armor, no defense against the blows of the enemy. You stand condemned already, needing Christ as your only refuge (John 3:18).

The Bible says, *"For the weapons of our warfare are not carnal, but mighty through God to the pulling down of strong holds"* (2 Corinthians 10:4). Notice the phrase: *"through God"*. The struggles you face will never be solved by willpower alone, or by trying harder, or by filling your mind with positive thoughts. These are spiritual problems, and they require spiritual power.

Here is the key: that power belongs only to those who belong to Christ.

Perhaps that is why your fight has seemed impossible. You have prayed, you have tried to change, you have even promised God you would do better, yet something is still missing. The truth is, you have been facing a spiritual enemy without the authority of Christ. And without Him, the battle will always leave you empty, frustrated, and defeated.

Here is the sobering reality. Whether you realize it or not, you are already in the war. From the moment you were born, a battle has been raging for your soul. You do not get to choose whether you are in it. You only get to choose which side you are on.

The devil knows it. He does not need you to curse God or throw away your Bible. He does not need you to become an atheist. All he needs is to keep you distracted, deceived, and distant from Christ. If he can whisper doubt into your heart, if he can pull your eyes off God, if he can fill your days with busyness and compromise, then he has already gained ground.

The Bible warns us: *"Be sober, be vigilant; because your adversary the devil, as a roaring lion, walketh about, seeking whom he may devour"* (1 Peter 5:8). Think about that image. A lion does not need to kill the whole herd. He only needs to catch the one that is weak, the one that is unguarded, the one that has wandered from safety. Without Christ, that is exactly where you stand, exposed to the enemy who wants to destroy your soul.

Make no mistake. There is no neutral ground. Jesus Himself said, *"He that is not with me is against me"* (Matthew 12:30). You cannot sit on the fence. You are either standing with Christ or standing against Him.

Here is the good news, and it changes everything: Jesus has already won. The victory has been settled. On the cross, Christ disarmed Satan, defeated sin, and conquered death. When you belong to Him, His victory becomes your victory.

We see this truth in the life of Peter. On the night Jesus was betrayed, the Lord said, *"Simon, Simon, behold, Satan hath desired to have you, that he may sift you as wheat: but I have prayed for thee, that thy faith fail not"* (Luke 22:31-32). Peter thought he was strong and even boasted that he would never deny Christ. Yet in his own strength he failed three times before the rooster crowed. The attack was real, the enemy's target was personal, and Peter learned that without Christ's power even the boldest disciple can fall.

It is not just individuals who collapse when they fight without God's presence. Entire groups can fall as well. In Joshua 7, Israel went up to battle against a small city called Ai. They thought it would be an easy victory, but because of hidden sin in the camp, they went without God's power and were soundly defeated. What should have been a simple win became a humiliating loss, all because they tried to fight without the Lord.

Both Peter and Israel remind us of the same truth: no matter how strong you feel, no matter how small the battle looks, if you fight without Christ's authority and presence you will fall. But when you belong to Him, His strength becomes your strength and His victory becomes your victory.

The enemy never rests because the stakes are eternal.

I have seen the same pattern repeat in the lives of Christians today. A man tries to overcome an addiction by gritting his teeth and promising to do better. A woman tries to control her fear by reading self-help books and repeating positive thoughts. A teenager tries to resist temptation by hiding it instead of confessing to it. For a while, it may look like they are winning, but sooner or later, their strength runs out. Why? Because you cannot fight a spiritual battle with fleshly

Chapter 1: Before You Fight, You Must Belong

weapons. Without Christ, the cycle repeats. With Him, the chains can be broken.

This brings us to the bigger question: why does the pressure feel so constant? Why does it feel like the enemy never lets up?

The Real Reason You Are Under Attack

A friend once asked me, *"Steve, why do I feel like I'm constantly under attack? Nothing I do seems to work, and I keep falling apart."*

Maybe you've felt the same. You take one step forward, but it feels like you're shoved two steps back. You try to hold things together, but no matter what you do, something keeps fighting against you.

Have you ever stopped and wondered why? Why does the pressure never let up, even when you're trying to do right? Why does the battle feel so relentless?

The answer is clear. It is because Satan hates God, and because you are made in God's image, he despises you. If you are lost, he works to blind you to the gospel. If you are saved, he works to oppose your walk with Christ. From the very beginning, the devil has set himself against everything that reflects God's glory. He could not overthrow the throne of heaven, so he wages war against the next best target, those who bear the image of the Creator. That includes you.

Make no mistake, his attacks are not random. The Bible tells us the thief has come *"to steal, and to kill, and to destroy"* (John 10:10). Satan wants to rob you of joy, strip you of peace, and crush your confidence in God. He knows that if he can keep you weak, distracted, and discouraged, you will not live out the calling God has placed on your life.

If you are not saved, his goal is simple: keep you blind to the truth of the gospel until it is too late. That is why Paul wrote, *"the god of this world hath blinded the minds of them which believe not"* (2 Corinthians 4:4). The devil is working to keep your eyes closed to Christ.

But if you are saved, his tactics shift. He cannot take your salvation, but he can take your effectiveness. He wants you silent when you should be speaking, fearful when you should be standing, and defeated when you should be walking in victory.

Spiritual Warfare: Building Your Battle Plan

That is why the battle feels so personal. Because it is personal. The enemy cannot hurt God directly, so he strikes at the heart of God's work by attacking those God loves. And that includes you. Whether you know Christ or not, you are in the battle, and the enemy has already set his sights on your soul.

**The battle is personal
because you are precious to God.**

What Does It Mean to Be Saved?

"Saved" is a word you often hear in church, but what does it really mean? Saved from what? And why does it matter?

To be saved means to be rescued: rescued from sin, rescued from separation from God, and rescued from eternal judgment. That is not a word to be taken lightly. Salvation is not a churchy label. It is a lifeline.

To fully understand what it means to be *"saved"*, we must first understand sin. Sin is not just the bad things other people do. Sin is disobeying God: in action, in thought, or even in motive. Sometimes sin is doing what God forbids, like lying, cheating, or stealing. Other times it is failing to do what God commands, like loving your neighbor, forgiving your enemy, or trusting Him fully. *"Therefore to him that knoweth to do good, and doeth it not, to him it is sin"* (James 4:17).

And sin always carries a consequence. Sin separates us from God in this life, leaving us guilty, restless, and ashamed. And if left unforgiven, sin leads to eternal judgment: eternal separation from God in hell (Luke 16:23). That is not just theology. It is reality. Deep down, your conscience has reminded you of it more times than you care to admit. Every feeling of guilt, every restless night, every unshakable fear of death, all of it points to the same truth: sin has a price.

Here is where many get confused. Some believe they are safe because they were baptized as a baby. Others think their faithful church attendance or family tradition is enough. Still others hope their good deeds will outweigh their bad. But none of these erase sin.

Chapter 1: Before You Fight, You Must Belong

Religion can polish the outside while leaving the heart unchanged. Baptism, membership, and morality cannot save. Only Christ can.

This is why salvation cannot be about self-improvement, religion, or good works. *"For by grace are ye saved through faith; and that not of yourselves: it is the gift of God: Not of works, lest any man should boast"* (Ephesians 2:8–9). You cannot erase your sin. You cannot climb your way back to God. You must be rescued.

That is exactly what Jesus Christ came to do. *"But God commendeth his love toward us, in that, while we were yet sinners, Christ died for us"* (Romans 5:8). Jesus did not wait for us to clean up our act. He did not demand that we prove ourselves worthy. He loved us at our worst. He took our place. On the cross, He bore the penalty of our sin, and by His resurrection, He opened the way for forgiveness and eternal life.

Think of it this way: you are like a drowning man in the ocean. No matter how hard you swim, the waves keep dragging you under. Religion might throw you a rulebook on how to swim better. Self-help might tell you to *"believe in yourself"* and kick harder. But none of that saves you. What you need is someone strong enough to reach into the water and pull you out. That is what Christ did. He did not come to hand you advice. He came to rescue your soul.

That is what it means to be saved: forgiven of sin, reconciled to God, and given eternal life through a personal relationship with Jesus Christ. That is the rescue every one of us needs, and the rescue God freely offers you today.

Salvation is not a label.
It is a lifeline.

How Can You Be Saved?

The Bible gives a clear and direct answer: *"That if thou shalt confess with thy mouth the Lord Jesus, and shalt believe in thine heart that God hath raised him from the dead, thou shalt be saved. For with the heart man believeth unto righteousness; and with the mouth confession is made unto salvation"* (Romans 10:9–10).

Spiritual Warfare: Building Your Battle Plan

Notice how simple and yet how serious this is. Salvation is not about reciting the right words or performing a ritual. It is about believing in your heart and turning to Christ in faith.

To be saved, three things must take place:

1. ***You must admit your need.*** You are a sinner who cannot save yourself. Scripture says, *"For all have sinned, and come short of the glory of God"* (Romans 3:23). That includes you. No amount of excuses or comparisons to others can erase that truth.

2. ***You must believe the gospel.*** Jesus died for your sins, was buried, and rose again. That is the heart of the good news. Paul declared it this way: *"Christ died for our sins according to the scriptures; and... he was buried, and... he rose again the third day according to the scriptures"* (1 Corinthians 15:3-4). The gospel is not advice. It is a finished work.

3. ***You must call on Him personally.*** Salvation is not automatic. It requires your personal response of faith. The Bible promises, *"For whosoever shall call upon the name of the Lord shall be saved"* (Romans 10:13). That means you. Not just the person next to you. Not just the preacher in the pulpit. Anyone who calls upon Christ in faith will be saved.

It really is that simple. Yet for some, it feels impossible. Maybe you have tried before. You have prayed, you have made promises to God, you have tried to turn over a new leaf. But this is different. This is not about what you can do for God. This is about what Christ has already done for you.

Think of the thief on the cross. He had nothing to offer: no chance to turn over a new leaf, no time to make up for his past. Yet, in his dying moments he turned to Jesus and said, *"Lord, remember me when thou comest into thy kingdom"* (Luke 23:42). And Jesus answered, *"Verily I say unto thee, Today shalt thou be with me in paradise"* (Luke 23:43). One cry of faith changed his eternity.

Chapter 1: Before You Fight, You Must Belong

So let me ask you. Have you ever truly called on Jesus to save you? Not just gone to church. Not just tried to be good. Have you personally turned to Him in repentance and faith?

If you are ready, you can settle it right now. The prayer itself does not save you. What saves is your faith in Christ. If you believe the gospel and you are ready to call upon Christ, you can pray something like this:

"Dear Lord, I confess that I am a sinner and I need to be saved. I believe that Jesus Christ is the Son of God, and that He died on the cross to pay for my sin and that He rose again on the third day. Forgive me of my sin, come into my heart, and save my soul. In Jesus' name, Amen."

If you belong to Christ, His victory is your victory.

If you truly called upon Christ in faith, then according to God's Word, you are saved forever. You now belong to Christ, and He has promised, *"I give unto them eternal life; and they shall never perish, neither shall any man pluck them out of my hand"* (John 10:28). His Spirit lives within you, His Word is your weapon, and His victory is your victory. Here is the assurance: salvation does not rest on your feelings, but on God's promise. Feelings change. Promises do not. *"He that believeth on the Son hath everlasting life"* (John 3:36).

This assurance matters deeply for the battle ahead. If you doubt your salvation, the enemy will use that doubt as a weapon. But when you know you belong to Christ, you fight from a place of confidence, not confusion. The devil wants you unsure, but God wants you settled. That certainty is your first shield in warfare.

You may not always feel different at first. Doubts may come. The devil will whisper, *"That prayer did not work,"* or *"You are not really saved."* But do not listen to his lies. Anchor your heart in God's Word. Jesus said, *"Verily, verily, I say unto you, He that heareth my word, and believeth on him that sent me, hath everlasting life, and shall not come into condemnation; but is passed from death unto life"* (John 5:24).

Spiritual Warfare: Building Your Battle Plan

That means if you have turned to Christ in faith, you can know beyond a shadow of a doubt that you are saved. It is not based on what you feel. It is not based on what you do tomorrow. It is based on what Christ has already done for you and the unchanging promise of God.

Now You Are Ready for Battle

If you have trusted Christ, you are no longer fighting alone. The Spirit of God now lives in you. He teaches you the truth of His Word, strengthens your faith, and gives you access to His power. You are not the same person you were before. You are a child of God, equipped for the fight ahead.

Maybe you just prayed and called upon Christ. If so, take courage. The battle is real, but so is the victory that belongs to you in Him. Salvation does not remove the fight; it gives you the armor to stand in it. Without Christ, you were defenseless. With Christ, you are armed and ready.

This book will now guide you, step by step, on how to stand strong when the spiritual attacks come. We will uncover the enemy's tactics. We will walk through God's promises. And we will learn how to fight in the strength of Christ instead of the weakness of our own flesh.

If you are still unsure, pause here. Do not move forward until you know for certain where you stand. Everything in this book depends on this one thing: you must belong to Christ before you can stand against the enemy. If you are not in Him, you will remain vulnerable. But if you are in Him, you are secure.

Do you see it now? You are not the victim; through Christ, you are the conqueror. *"Nay, in all these things we are more than conquerors through him that loved us"* (Romans 8:37). That is your starting point. That is your confidence. That is the victory you now walk in.

Through Christ,
You are more than a conqueror!

Chapter 1: Before You Fight, You Must Belong

Building Your Battle Plan

Congratulations! You have finished the first chapter, and that is not a small task. You haven't learned tactics yet. You haven't been given moves, counters, or instructions. But you have already confronted something far more important. You have faced the question of where you belong. Before any strategy is formed, before any resistance is made, before any stand is taken against the enemy, which side you are on must be settled. War is never accidental. Sides must be chosen first.

What comes next is not a wrap-up. It is a transition. At the end of every chapter, you'll hit something deliberate, something with structure, designed to tie what you've just learned to the next step you'll take. These sections are called *"Build Your Battle Plan."* They exist so what you have just read does not remain abstract or unresolved but begins to take shape with intent and direction.

This first battle plan locks in on exactly where we have left off, who you belong to. Every single thing coming after this in the book is built on that ground. You are not moving forward guessing or reacting on emotion alone. You are preparing to stand with awareness, resolve, and purpose. What follows establishes the pattern for the chapters ahead and the fight you are stepping into.

1

BUILD YOUR BATTLE PLAN

CHOOSE YOUR SIDE

Before we push any further, there's one question that must be settled, right now. Not somewhere down the road, not little by little, and definitely not just assumed.

Do you belong to Christ?

This isn't some gentle prompt for reflection. It's the line that decides everything else. Spiritual warfare doesn't begin with better awareness or more effort. It starts with life, His life in you. Without Christ, there's no ground to stand on, no authority to speak from, and no real protection. The fight we just talked about in this chapter is absolutely real, but you can't step into it apart from Him.

That's why this first Battle Plan isn't about gearing up for war yet. It's about making sure you're on the right side.

Take whatever time you need with what comes next. Don't brush it off like a checkbox or a formality. Nothing in the rest of this book will help at all if this one question stays unsettled.

Step 1: Settle the Question of Belonging

Answer the question directly, without qualification.

Right now, I can say with certainty that I belong to Christ:

☐ Yes
☐ No
☐ I am not sure

Do not answer based on what you hope is true, what you have always assumed, or what others think. Answer based on what you actually know in your heart.

Step 2: If You Know You Belong to Christ

If you answered **Yes**, take the time to put it into words right now. This isn't about stirring up emotion or crafting some inspiring story. It's about getting clear. One of the main ways doubt creeps in is when what you know to be true stays vague and unspoken. Writing this down establishes an anchor in your faith. It gives you something concrete to return to when you begin to doubt.

So, in your own words, write down how you came to belong to Christ.

My Salvation Testimony:
When did I trust Christ?

Where was I when this took place?

What did I understand about my need to be saved?

What did I understand about my need to be saved?

What did I believe about Jesus Christ at that time?
(His death, burial, and resurrection)

How did I personally respond to Him?

If you're not absolutely sure, don't ignore that feeling. Settle it once and for all, right now. Go back to Chapter 1. Read it slowly. Walk through the gospel again. Look up every verse. Speak to the Lord out loud if you need to. Call on Him. Make it real and certain today.

If this book is what God used to bring you to Christ, praise the Lord! I'm genuinely thrilled for you. You have just made the single most important decision anyone can ever make. I have a gift I want to send you. If you would let me know, I would count it a privilege to rejoice with you and help you take your next steps.

Please visit this link and let us know:
http://www.canadachurchplanting.com/free-gift
You are not alone. We want to celebrate with you and help you grow.

Step 3: Final Reflection

In one or two sentences, answer these questions.

How does knowing you belong to Christ change the way you view spiritual warfare?

What verse from Chapter 1 do you want to hold onto when the enemy tries to make you doubt your salvation?

PART TWO

THE ATTACK

*When the enemy strikes,
awareness is the beginning of victory*

2

RECOGNIZING THE ATTACK

What you call coincidence may be the enemy's camouflage.

Have you ever had a day when everything seemed to go wrong? Not just a rough morning, but a day that felt like the whole world was against you. You woke up feeling fine and promised yourself it would be a good day. But then the car wouldn't start. Traffic made you late. The boss was upset. Then the phone rang with bad news, your child was sick. One thing after another, until it felt like the whole day was falling apart. You checked the clock and it was only noon.

That may be more than a coincidence. That may be a spiritual attack.

If you miss that it's spiritual, you'll blame your spouse, your boss, or what feels like bad luck. You'll fight people, bills, or feelings, while the real enemy stays hidden. That's why recognition matters.

Missing the spiritual side
leaves you fighting the wrong enemy.

Spiritual Warfare: Building Your Battle Plan

Job: A Man Caught in the Middle of War

One of the clearest pictures of spiritual attack is found in the life of Job. His story doesn't start with rebellion or compromise. It starts in heaven: *"And the LORD said unto Satan, Hast thou considered my servant Job, that there is none like him in the earth, a perfect and an upright man, one that feareth God, and escheweth evil?"* (Job 1:8).

Unknowingly, Job's name came up in a spiritual conversation between God and Satan. Satan accused Job of fearing God only because of the blessings around him, saying that if those were stripped away, Job would curse God to His face. In response, God set the limits and permitted the testing, for Satan could go no further than God allowed. And in a single day, Job lost everything (Job 1:9–12).

The oxen and donkeys were stolen, the sheep consumed by fire, the camels raided, and the servants slain. His ten children were crushed in one windstorm. *"While he was yet speaking, there came also another..."* (Job 1:16).

Wave after wave, loss after loss, no pause, no explanation, no chance to recover. That is what a full-force spiritual attack looks like.

Job's story is not just history on a page. You may not lose camels or herds, but you know what it feels like when the blows keep coming, one phone call with bad news, then a bill you can't pay, then conflict with someone you love. Like Job, you may not hear the heavenly conversation, but you feel the earthly impact.

I've counseled believers going through seasons just like that. One family in our church seemed to have everything hit at once. The husband lost his job. The wife got sick. The car broke down. Bills piled up. They came to me confused, asking, *"Pastor, what are we doing wrong?"* But when we looked at the timing, it lined up with them getting serious about serving God, tithing faithfully, sharing their faith. It wasn't punishment. It was resistance.

Job shows us how attacks can strike every part of life at once, but always within God's limits.

Chapter 2: Recognizing the Attack

Why Recognition Matters

That raises the question for you: How do you know when you're under attack?

Life has its challenges and its share of problems. But sometimes when life's problems come from every direction all at once without explanation, it may be a sign that something spiritual is happening beyond what you can see.

If you fail to recognize it, you'll assume it's a mere coincidence or bad luck. You'll fight the wrong battles, wasting strength on people or circumstances, while the real enemy stays hidden. Recognizing it as a spiritual attack pulls back the curtain and exposes the devil's involvement.

Paul warns, *"Lest Satan should get an advantage of us: for we are not ignorant of his devices"* (2 Corinthians 2:11). The danger is not how clever Satan is, but how unaware we can be. We're quick to blame others, dodge the truth, or take offense too easily. When we do, we hand Satan the advantage.

That is why this chapter matters. If you can learn to see where and how the enemy attacks, you will stop wasting your energy in the wrong fight. Recognition isn't the victory itself, but it is the first step toward standing strong in Christ, who gives the victory. (Ephesians 6:10–11; 1 Corinthians 15:57).

Ignorance gives the enemy advantage.
Recognition takes it back.

The Enemy's Common Ground

Job's story reveals that spiritual attacks can strike every part of life simultaneously, but always within the limits God allows (Job 1:12). Scripture, and often our own lives, show us that the enemy often targets the same areas again and again. These are the places where believers most often feel the weight of the fight.

In the pages ahead, we'll look at six areas where the enemy strikes: physically, emotionally, financially, relationally, mentally, and spiritually.

Spiritual Warfare: Building Your Battle Plan

Your life may not mirror Job's, but you may see yourself in these patterns. And once you do, you'll be prepared to face what comes next.

Physically: When the Body Becomes a Battlefield

One of the most common battlefields in spiritual warfare is the body itself. We often assume the enemy only attacks through temptation or fear, but at times, as in Job's case, he is allowed to afflict the body, leaving you too weak to pray, too weary to read, and too exhausted to worship (Job 2:7).

Sometimes it happens suddenly, a cough, a slight fever, a pounding headache. Other times it leaves you feeling exhausted and completely drained of all your energy. Or worse, it comes as a series of injuries or setbacks. Such hindrances can be meant to keep you out of church, and strangely, they almost always appear right before Sunday morning.

Biblical Examples

After Job lost his children and possessions, Satan struck again: "So went Satan forth from the presence of the LORD, and smote Job with sore boils from the sole of his foot unto his crown" (Job 2:7).

This was not just a natural illness but a direct spiritual attack on Job's body that robbed him of both his strength and his appearance. The suffering was so severe that his wife urged him to *"curse God, and die"* (Job 2:9). This physical pain was a weapon the enemy meant to use against Job's faith, but only within the boundaries God permitted.

We see the same principle in the New Testament. Paul spoke of his *"thorn in the flesh, the messenger of Satan to buffet me"* (2 Corinthians 12:7). Just as Job's boils were physical pain permitted by God, Paul's thorn was also a physical affliction delivered through satanic attack. Yet God used it with purpose. It humbled Paul, kept him dependent on grace, and turned what the enemy meant for harm into a testimony of God's strength.

Even Elijah felt the toll on his body after his great victory on Mount Carmel. Soon after, he collapsed under a juniper tree, exhausted, discouraged, and praying for death (1 Kings 19:4). His

Chapter 2: Recognizing the Attack

weakness shows how physical exhaustion can open the door for discouragement, a battlefield where the enemy seeks to take advantage.

Modern Examples

Think of the faithful deacon who serves tirelessly in his church, yet suddenly faces one health issue after another. Doctors find no clear cause, yet the timing always seems to coincide with moments after spiritual victories. Or consider the young mother who wakes up early to spend time in her Bible, only to struggle with crushing migraines that appear without warning.

I even remember a family that never missed a service, slowly worn down through repeated illnesses. One week it was the mother sick, the next a child, then the father. Urgent care visits piled up, their attendance slipped, and before long they had missed so much church that they no longer missed being in church.

We must remember that not every sickness is a spiritual attack. Yet when the body is struck again and again without clear cause, especially during seasons of spiritual victory, it may be more than coincidence.

This is how the enemy works: he seeks to wear down your body so that your faith might fade, but God's grace is sufficient, and His strength is made perfect in weakness (2 Corinthians 12:9; Ephesians 6:10–11).

Why the Enemy Strikes the Body

The enemy knows the body is the servant of the soul. When your body is strong, it is easier to pray, reading Scripture feels natural, and worship flows freely. But when the body fails, discouragement soon follows. Satan knows that weakness of the flesh often opens the door to weakness of faith.

A weary body makes it harder to fight temptation. A sick body makes it harder to attend worship. A broken body makes it easier to doubt God's goodness. This is why Paul warned the Corinthians: *"Know ye not that your body is the temple of the Holy Ghost which is*

Spiritual Warfare: Building Your Battle Plan

in you... and ye are not your own?" (1 Corinthians 6:19). If the body is God's temple, then the enemy has every reason to attack it.

The Danger of Misdiagnosis

If you misdiagnose a physical attack, two dangers follow. First, you may shrug it off as *"just bad luck,"* never realizing the enemy is deliberately seeking to wear you down. Second, you may treat every illness as a spiritual attack, neglecting medical care or needed rest. Both errors are costly.

Job's boils were real. Paul's thorn was real. Elijah's exhaustion was real. Scripture shows each case honestly for what it was, and wisdom is needed to discern whether an illness is simply physical or whether it carries the marks of a spiritual attack.

Recognition

How do you recognize when your body is under a spiritual attack? Often, it comes in sudden, unexpected waves: sickness, exhaustion, or injuries that multiply without a clear cause and frequently appear just before or just after a period of spiritual growth or ministry success. Recognizing the situation helps you seek God's wisdom to discern whether it is simply a cold or a spiritual attack.

Job's boils show us how physical suffering can be weaponized. But the enemy does not stop with the body. He continues further into the emotions that flow from that suffering.

The enemy strikes the body to weaken the soul.

Emotionally: When the Heart Is Overwhelmed

If the enemy cannot break you down physically, he will often attack you through your emotions. Fear, anger, discouragement, or sudden sadness can arise without explanation. At times, the enemy seizes on these moments and turns them into attacks, arriving without warning, without clear cause, and often without an answer.

Chapter 2: Recognizing the Attack

This is one of the devil's most subtle battlegrounds, because emotions feel so real and powerful. Fear whispers lies, telling you that you are helpless, alone, or trapped, yet God has said, *"I will never leave thee, nor forsake thee"* (Hebrews 13:5). Despair tempts you to believe that God has abandoned you, but His Word assures, *"The LORD is nigh unto them that are of a broken heart"* (Psalm 34:18). Anger consumes you and leads to rage, but the Spirit calls us to put away *"anger, wrath, malice"* (Colossians 3:8). That is why you must test your emotions rather than accept them at face value.

Biblical Examples

David wrestled with his emotions. In Psalm 42:5 he cries, *"Why art thou cast down, O my soul? and why art thou disquieted in me? hope thou in God."* His despair had no rational explanation. There was no visible enemy, no immediate crisis. It came from within, heavy and unshakable. Yet David refused to accept it as final. He spoke to his own soul and commanded it to hope in God.

Elijah's emotional crash followed his physical collapse, as we saw earlier. After fire fell on Mount Carmel and the prophets of Baal were defeated, he fled into the wilderness, terrified of Jezebel's threat. He sat under a juniper tree and begged for death: *"It is enough; now, O LORD, take away my life"* (1 Kings 19:4). His emotions overwhelmed him until God restored him step by step.

Even the disciples, walking with Christ, felt their hearts seized by fear in the storm: *"Master, carest thou not that we perish?"* (Mark 4:38). Their panic didn't come from the storm alone. It came from fear clouding their faith, the very kind of fear the enemy loves to exploit.

Modern Examples

Emotional attacks are just as real today. A young believer wakes up with anxiety, even though nothing is wrong. A faithful father finds himself quick-tempered and irritable, lashing out at those he loves most. A teenager feels isolated and unwanted, even though friends and family surround them.

I've even walked through this myself. The very week I surrendered

Spiritual Warfare: Building Your Battle Plan

to God's call to ministry, panic gripped me so badly that I was in and out of hospitals for months. Fear convinced me I was dying, that a heart attack or stroke was imminent. I saw doctor after doctor, and medical bills piled up to an overwhelming amount. But the real battle wasn't in my body. It was fear. That is what an emotional attack can look like: panic, stress, and overwhelming anxiety, the very feelings the enemy loves to magnify in order to cloud faith.

Why the Enemy Strikes the Heart

The enemy knows that your emotions affect everything else. Fear shrinks your faith. Anger poisons your relationships. Sadness drains your energy. If Satan can twist your emotions, he can twist your perception of God and others.

That is why Scripture warns us: *"Be ye angry, and sin not: let not the sun go down upon your wrath: Neither give place to the devil"* (Ephesians 4:26–27). Anger left unchecked is not just unhealthy. It is a foothold for the enemy.

The same is true with fear. Paul reminded Timothy, *"For God hath not given us the spirit of fear; but of power, and of love, and of a sound mind"* (2 Timothy 1:7). Fear can take control of your thoughts and decisions. Some have described fear this way: F.E.A.R., *"false evidence appearing real."* It's just a saying, but it illustrates how the enemy uses fear to cloud truth and form lies in our minds.

The Danger of Misdiagnosis

If you fail to recognize an emotional attack, you will likely mislabel yourself. You begin to say, *"I'm just an anxious person. I'm just angry by nature. I'm just too sensitive."* In time, you accept an identity the enemy crafted instead of remembering who you are in Christ.

On the other hand, if you blame every mood swing on Satan, you avoid taking responsibility for habits that need change. Sometimes sadness is simply grief. Sometimes fear is the body's natural response. Wisdom comes in noticing when emotions arrive with unusual intensity, persist without clear reason, or directly oppose the truth of God's Word. When that happens, you are likely facing more than

Chapter 2: Recognizing the Attack

ordinary emotions. You are facing a spiritual battle.

Recognition

Recognizing an emotional attack does not mean pretending your feelings aren't real. It means being honest about the weight you carry and alert to the possibility of the enemy behind it. It is noticing when your emotions get out of control or when feelings become so overwhelming that they cloud your view of God. Recognition begins with this question: Are these simply my emotions, or is the enemy seeking to use them against me? That question redirects your focus back to God, asking Him to reveal the difference.

When your emotions are overwhelmed, it affects every part of life. But the enemy does not stop with your emotions. He often focuses next on your finances, because he knows how quickly money troubles can steal joy, stir fear, and divide homes.

The enemy strikes the heart because emotions shape everything else.

Financially: When Resources Collapse

Financial struggles often reveal spiritual attack more quickly than anything else. Why? Because money touches nearly every aspect of life. It touches your meals, your bills, and your ability to give. That's why the Bible is so clear: *"the love of money is the root of all evil"* (1 Timothy 6:10). Notice, Scripture does not say money itself is evil. Money is a tool. But when love for money takes hold of the heart, it opens the door for pride, greed, and every kind of sin.

The enemy knows this, and he uses it. If he can take advantage of financial problems, he can quickly instill fear in your heart and sow doubt in your mind. This type of attack shows up in your grocery cart and your offering plate. At its core, the enemy uses it to make you doubt that God will provide.

Spiritual Warfare: Building Your Battle Plan

Biblical Examples

Job's wealth was stripped in a single day. The oxen and donkeys were stolen, the sheep were consumed by fire, the camels were raided, and the servants were slain (Job 1:14-17). His entire livelihood collapsed wave after wave. This was not poor management. It was a direct spiritual assault.

Haggai describes how God sometimes withholds prosperity to correct His people: *"Ye have sown much, and bring in little... and he that earneth wages earneth wages to put it into a bag with holes"* (Haggai 1:6). While not every financial struggle is spiritual attack, the Bible shows that sometimes God allows financial lack for correction, and sometimes Satan attacks through it.

In the New Testament, Paul warned that Satan seeks to *"get an advantage"* (2 Corinthians 2:11). What better way than to strike where people feel most vulnerable, their daily bread and security? Yet even here, God reminds us that He is the true provider (Matthew 6:31–33; Philippians 4:19).

Modern Examples

A man faithfully tithes, but just as he commits to giving more, his hours at work are cut. A couple saves diligently, but the week they decide to support a missionary, both the car and the furnace break down. A young family lives within their means, yet wave after wave of unexpected bills leaves them drained and tempted to question whether God still cares.

I've watched this happen more times than I can count. Someone gets saved, follows the Lord in baptism, and is in church every service. They are on fire for the Lord. Then what seems to be an answer to their prayers comes. They get that new job. Better pay, better hours, but it takes them out of church on Sundays. They take it, convinced God answered their prayer. But let me ask you this question. Do you think God will give you a job if that means taking you completely out of the church?

No! That wasn't the Lord providing. That was the enemy luring them in, and they took the bait. Sadly, weeks turn into months, and

Chapter 2: Recognizing the Attack

the fire for God is extinguished. And often enough, they end up leaving that job, but they never return to the church. You see, the enemy's goal wasn't only to hurt them, but to deceive them, and they fell for it.

> **Better hours and better pay mean nothing if they cost you your walk with God.**

Financial attacks often show up in clusters, not just one bill, but several. Not just one breakdown, but many. Not just one loss, but a cascade that feels timed to discourage faith.

Why the Enemy Strikes Finances

The enemy knows that money problems expose the heart. Jesus said, *"For where your treasure is, there will your heart be also"* (Matthew 6:21). That is why the enemy often seeks to strike believers in the area of their needs, because money problems quickly reveal whether we are trusting God or ourselves.

When the bills cost more than your paycheck, fear rises and whispers that God will not see you through. When the numbers don't add up, doubt creeps in and questions whether God truly provides. When money grows tight, arguments often follow in the marriage and ripple through the home. When others prosper while you struggle, bitterness hardens the heart just as it did for Asaph when he envied *"the prosperity of the wicked"* (Psalm 73:3).

Remember the enemy's aim is not your finances. It is your faith. He wants you to believe that God cannot be trusted. Yet the Word of God declares, *"But my God shall supply all your need according to his riches in glory by Christ Jesus"* (Philippians 4:19).

> **Financial attacks aim at your faith, not just your wallet.**

The Danger of Misdiagnosis

If you assume every financial problem is only poor budgeting, you may miss seasons where the enemy is intentionally attacking your finances

Spiritual Warfare: Building Your Battle Plan

to weaken your trust in God. On the other hand, if you blame every setback on Satan, you avoid taking responsibility for poor stewardship. Sometimes, financial pain is the result of foolish spending, neglect of stewardship, or a failure to work diligently.

Recognition means asking the tough question. Is this simply the result of my choices, or is there a pattern of opposition that shows up right after a spiritual victory? If the timing, intensity, and repetition seem designed to weaken your faith, it may be more than a budget issue. It may be a spiritual attack.

Recognition

Recognizing when you are under a financial attack requires both honest self-examination and spiritual discernment. Sometimes, financial stress is simply the result of poor decisions, but at other times, the timing and weight reveal something more. When setbacks come one after another, like waves, when the financial problems come right after spiritual victory, or when the struggle feels aimed at shaking your trust in God's provision, you may be facing more than ordinary financial problems. You may be under attack.

Job not only lost his wealth, but he also faced conflict at home. His wife urged him to *"curse God, and die"* (Job 2:9). The enemy who seeks to strip away your livelihood will often move next to destroy your closest relationships.

Relationally: When People Become the Battleground

Another common area of spiritual attack is in our relationships. Scripture reminds us, *"we wrestle not against flesh and blood"* (Ephesians 6:12). That means people are not your enemy, even though the true enemy can make it feel like they are. Sometimes, the very people you trust most, those closest to your heart, can become the battlefield the enemy uses to isolate you.

Family, friendships, and the fellowship of the church are meant to be places of safety and strength. When the devil stirs strife, those same places can quickly turn into sources of pain. An argument at home can hurt deeper than a stranger's insult. Division in the church can drain

Chapter 2: Recognizing the Attack

more strength than persecution from the outside. That is why Scripture warns, *"Neither give place to the devil"* (Ephesians 4:27).

Conflict at home, division among friends, or discord in the church are never small matters. More often than we realize, they are spiritual attacks, designed to discourage even the most faithful believer and to weaken the strongest church.

Satan knows that if he can divide God's people, he can weaken their testimony and silence their witness. That is why Paul warned the Corinthians about the need for forgiveness: *'Lest Satan should get an advantage of us: for we are not ignorant of his devices'* (2 Corinthians 2:11).

Biblical Examples

Job's wife, broken by grief, lashed out at him: *"Dost thou still retain thine integrity? curse God, and die"* (Job 2:9). In many ways, those words cut deeper than the boils on his skin. The enemy had not only stripped Job's wealth and health; he was now driving a wedge into Job's most intimate relationship. What should have been a source of comfort became a weapon of pain.

Job was not alone in this experience. The psalmist described the same pain when he wrote of betrayal by a close friend (Psalm 41:9). Few wounds cut deeper than betrayal by a friend. The sting of an enemy hurts, but the betrayal of a loved one goes straight to the soul.

This pattern is also evident in the New Testament. Paul knew this sorrow. He wrote of Demas: *"For Demas hath forsaken me, having loved this present world"* (2 Timothy 4:10). Later he added, *"At my first answer no man stood with me, but all men forsook me"* (v.16). The great apostle was not undone by Rome alone, but also by the abandonment of those he had counted on to stand with him. The battle was not only outside the church walls. It was among those he once trusted.

Modern Examples

A marriage begins to fall apart, not from one great betrayal but from a series of small misunderstandings that the enemy fans into flame. A church member becomes offended by a minor issue and leaves the church, leaving fellowship broken.

The same pattern shows up in churches. I know of a church where it started small. One member felt overlooked. Another thought leadership didn't listen. A whisper here, an offense there. What should have been a minor issue, easily resolved, turned into suspicion and gossip. Soon sides were taken, and friendships that once were strong grew cold. In the end, it wasn't about the original issue anymore. It was about wounded pride and broken trust, which ultimately led to a church split. What began as a small misunderstanding became Satan's weapon, exploiting pride and offense to tear apart an entire body of believers.

That's the danger of relational attacks: they rarely stay small. Left unchecked, they spread like wildfire, just as James warns, *"the tongue is a fire, a world of iniquity"* (James 3:6). Careless words, spoken in anger or offense, can burn down what took years to build, until a marriage is ruined or a church is divided.

Regardless of the setting, the enemy's strategy does not change. He delights in turning allies into adversaries, magnifying small offenses, and sowing seeds of suspicion. The very places meant to be a refuge, the home, the church, the family of God, become a battlefield.

Why the Enemy Strikes Relationships

Relationships are God's design for strength. Solomon wrote, *"Two are better than one; because they have a good reward for their labour. For if they fall, the one will lift up his fellow"* (Ecclesiastes 4:9–10). Satan knows this. He also knows that *"a house divided against itself shall not stand"* (Mark 3:25).

That is why the enemy works so hard to sow division. He magnifies careless words until they cut like weapons (Proverbs 12:18). He whispers lies into the cracks of trust. Once unity breaks, strength collapses, and discouragement quickly follows.

Think about it. Conflict at home leaves you praying through tears. Strife within the church can leave you distracted from worship. Betrayal by a friend leaves you doubting everyone.

Yet the truth remains: people are not your enemy. Satan wants you

Chapter 2: Recognizing the Attack

to think they are. Paul reminds us that our battle is never with people but with the unseen enemy working behind the scenes (Ephesians 6:12).

Relational attacks turn allies into adversaries to isolate and weaken you.

The Danger of Misdiagnosis

If you believe your spouse, your pastor, or your friend is the enemy, you are wasting your strength fighting the wrong battle. Instead of resisting the devil, you'll turn on the very people God placed in your life to help you.

On the other hand, if you refuse to admit that division is spiritual, you may excuse bitterness, gossip, or coldness as *"just the way relationships are."* Both errors keep the enemy's hand hidden.

Recognition

Recognizing relational attack means stepping back to ask: Why has this conflict escalated so quickly? Why does this offense feel so heavy? And why does this division occur right when God is at work?

When tension escalates beyond what the situation deserves, when a minor issue suddenly feels unbearable, or when unity breaks just as spiritual progress is being made, you may be facing more than ordinary conflict. You may be seeing the enemy exploiting human weakness, just as Peter warns us: *"Be sober, be vigilant; because your adversary the devil, as a roaring lion, walketh about, seeking whom he may devour"* (1 Peter 5:8). His goal is always the same: to divide, to isolate, and to weaken the testimony of God's people.

When relationships fall apart, the mind often spirals into chaos. Sleepless nights, racing thoughts, and constant distractions are signs that the next battlefield is being drawn: your thoughts and focus.

Spiritual Warfare: Building Your Battle Plan

Mentally: When the Mind Is Under Attack

The mind is one of the enemy's favorite battlefields, because what happens in your thoughts will soon shape your life. Scripture tells us, *"For as he thinketh in his heart, so is he"* (Proverbs 23:7). What you dwell on, whether worry, doubt, or hope, will eventually direct your steps.

That truth explains why Satan works so hard to plant lies, magnify fears, and cloud your judgment. God calls us to renew our minds (Romans 12:2) and to take every thought captive in Christ (2 Corinthians 10:5).

When your mind is under attack, even simple thoughts begin to scatter, and your focus slips, making decisions that once felt clear suddenly seem impossible. Soon, confusion settles in like a fog, and that fog turns every choice into a burden.

Biblical Examples

Job experienced this in his grief. He said, *"Therefore I will not refrain my mouth; I will speak in the anguish of my spirit; I will complain in the bitterness of my soul"* (Job 7:11). His thoughts spiraled out of control, racing with questions and bitterness until they spilled into words he could not restrain. In that moment, his mind, not just his body, became the battlefield.

Paul warned of the same danger: *"But I fear, lest by any means, as the serpent beguiled Eve through his subtilty, so your minds should be corrupted from the simplicity that is in Christ"* (2 Corinthians 11:3). Notice: Eve's downfall did not begin with her hand reaching for the fruit, but with a single thought of doubt planted in her mind.

Isaiah described the turmoil of those who refuse God as restless and unsettled, likening them to a troubled sea (Isaiah 57:20). A restless, unsettled mind is like that sea, constantly churning, easily stirred, and more vulnerable to the enemy's lies.

Whether in Job's sorrow, Eve's temptation, or the restless sea Isaiah described, the lesson is the same: when the mind is not set on God, it becomes vulnerable to attack.

Chapter 2: Recognizing the Attack

Modern Examples

A believer sits down to read the Bible, yet their thoughts scatter before they finish the first verse. Another kneels to pray, but distractions intrude within seconds. A student tries to study for an exam, only to battle racing thoughts of failure and despair.

I've sat across from believers who love the Lord but feel like their own mind has turned against them. They open the Bible, but as soon as their eyes hit the page, their thoughts scatter, to bills, chores, and worries that will not let go. They kneel to pray, but instead of peace, their mind fills with noise, lies, and distractions until the prayer ends in frustration and silence.

I've counseled students who break down in tears because every time they try to study or serve, a voice in their head whispers, *"You're a failure. You'll never get it right."* Those whispers do not come from nowhere. They echo the same lies Satan has always planted, from Eve in the garden to Job in his grief, and they are often amplified by the weakness of our flesh (Galatians 5:17) and the pull of this world (1 John 2:16). That is what it looks like when the mind is under attack.

Of course, mental fog can be caused by exhaustion, illness, or stress. But when it strikes suddenly, persists unnaturally, or consistently interrupts spiritual focus, it carries the fingerprints of the enemy. At that point, it is no longer a mere circumstance. It is a spiritual attack on the mind.

Why the Enemy Strikes the Mind

The enemy targets the mind because your thoughts shape your direction. What fills the mind will eventually shape the heart, the words, and the actions (Proverbs 23:7). If Satan can plant lies in the mind, he can poison the heart. If he can cloud your thinking, he can steer your steps. If he can keep your thoughts restless, he can keep your life fruitless.

That is why so many attacks begin as thoughts, doubts about God's goodness, lies about your worth, or fears about the future. If left unchallenged, those thoughts take root, and soon they govern your choices.

Spiritual Warfare: Building Your Battle Plan

This is why Paul wrote, "*Casting down imaginations, and every high thing that exalteth itself against the knowledge of God, and bringing into captivity every thought to the obedience of Christ*" (2 Corinthians 10:5). The mind is not a minor issue in spiritual warfare; it is the front line. The enemy knows it, and God's Word calls us to guard it.

The Danger of Misdiagnosis

Sometimes believers misdiagnose the battle in their mind. If you assume constant confusion is just personality, or that racing thoughts are just *"normal stress,"* you may miss the enemy's fingerprints. When distraction becomes a pattern that steals your focus from prayer, Scripture, and worship, it may be more than human weakness. It may be a spiritual attack.

The opposite mistake is just as dangerous. If you treat every distraction as an attack, you risk paranoia. Not every moment of forgetfulness or stress is from the enemy. Sometimes the mind is simply tired, and rest is what God prescribes.

Wisdom is found in knowing the difference. And God promises it: "*If any of you lack wisdom, let him ask of God, that giveth to all men liberally*" (James 1:5). When mental fog consistently pulls you away from God and His Word, discernment will show you whether it is fatigue or the enemy at work.

Recognition

Recognizing a mental spiritual attack means paying attention to patterns. Does your mind function clearly in daily tasks, yet suddenly scatter the moment you open Scripture or kneel to pray? Do uninvited doubts and lies intrude most often when you take a step of obedience or move closer to God? These are signs the enemy may be pressing hard on the mind.

Pay close attention to the timing. Attacks often reveal themselves by the timing of the strike. The mental fog that comes only during spiritual moments is rarely a coincidence. When confusion rises just as truth is read, or when distraction intensifies just as prayer begins,

Chapter 2: Recognizing the Attack

it may be more than fatigue. It may be a spiritual attack.

This is where the danger lies. When the mind is clouded, fellowship with God soon feels distant, though His presence has not left you (Hebrews 13:5). Confusion in thought often produces dryness in devotion. This is why the battlefield of the mind is sacred: the enemy does not only seek to distract your thoughts, but to disrupt your intimacy with God Himself.

The mind is the front line.
Guard it well.

Spiritually: When God Feels Distant

The deepest battleground of all is the spiritual life itself. Every other attack, including those on the body, emotions, finances, relationships, and the mind, ultimately aims here. The enemy's ultimate goal is not just to make you sick, discouraged, broke, lonely, or confused. His goal is to use those pressures to drive a wedge between you and God.

If he can make you feel abandoned, unheard, or empty in prayer, then he has struck at the very core of your walk. That silence in prayer, that dryness in worship, that false sense of distance, these are often the enemy's sharpest weapons, designed to convince you that God has stepped away when, in truth, He has not, for He has promised, *"I will never leave thee, nor forsake thee"* (Hebrews 13:5).

Biblical Examples

Job groaned, *"Behold, I go forward, but he is not there; and backward, but I cannot perceive him"* (Job 23:8). In the middle of his trial, Job could not sense God's presence. Everywhere he turned, he felt empty. Every prayer seemed unanswered. Every step gave the impression of being forsaken. His greatest pain was not the loss of wealth or health, but the silence of God.

Job was not alone in this struggle. David expressed the same anguish: *"Why standest thou afar off, O LORD? why hidest thou thyself in times of trouble?"* (Psalm 10:1). When spiritual attack

Spiritual Warfare: Building Your Battle Plan

strikes, even the strongest believer can feel abandoned by the very God who promised never to leave.

This cry is repeated again in the Psalms. *"My tears have been my meat day and night, while they continually say unto me, Where is thy God?"* (Psalm 42:3). That taunting question, *"Where is your God?"* is one the enemy loves to whisper, twisting pain into unbelief and driving the heart away from God.

Modern Examples

A believer opens the Bible and prepares to read, but the words feel flat and lifeless. A prayer warrior begins to pray, but their prayers seem to be going nowhere. A young believer who once burned with zeal suddenly feels cold and detached from God.

I've walked with believers through this very struggle. I once counseled a young woman who sat across from me with tears running down her cheeks. *"I've prayed night and day,"* she said, *"but it feels like I've fallen into a hole I can't climb out of. I want God, but I can't feel Him."* Over the next few weeks, she stopped answering calls, missed church, and withdrew from family and friends. The loneliness continued to grow worse until it became depression.

Her story is far from unique. In fact, it is becoming increasingly common among believers. This is often how spiritual attacks work. It steals the sense of God's presence, isolates you from others, and drags you toward despair. Even when you feel abandoned, the truth is that nothing can separate you from God. *"For I am persuaded, that neither death, nor life... nor any other creature, shall be able to separate us from the love of God"* (Romans 8:38–39).

Of course, not every season of dryness is a spiritual attack. Sometimes it comes naturally during seasons of growth and testing. But when dryness strikes again and again, or when it overlaps with physical, emotional, or relational strain, it may be more than circumstance. Iit may be the enemy attacking your fellowship with God.

Chapter 2: Recognizing the Attack

Why the Enemy Strikes the Spirit

Satan's ultimate strategy is to convince you that God has abandoned you. If he succeeds, he can unravel everything else. Here's how that lie works: a believer who doubts God's presence will soon begin to doubt His promises. A believer who feels forsaken, though God has not forsaken them, will soon forsake prayer. A believer who feels unloved will soon withhold love.

That is why Scripture calls us to lift the shield of faith. Paul urged the Ephesians, *"Above all, taking the shield of faith, wherewith ye shall be able to quench all the fiery darts of the wicked"* (Ephesians 6:16). Faith shields the spirit when feelings falter. The enemy's darts are not aimed only at the body or mind. They are designed to pierce the heart of trust in God Himself.

> **Spiritual attacks aim at your fellowship with God.**

The Danger of Misdiagnosis

If you assume dryness in prayer or Bible reading is just laziness, you may bury yourself under needless guilt. If you assume it is always God's punishment, you may sink into hopelessness. And if you assume it is always Satan, you may miss the seasons when God is using silence to stretch and deepen your faith.

Discernment is essential, because each cause requires a different response. If the dryness is from your own neglect, the answer is repentance and renewed discipline. If God has allowed a season of silence to refine you, the answer is patience and trust in His unseen work. But if the enemy is sowing confusion and mental heaviness, the answer is resistance, standing firm in the promises of God.

The wisdom lies in learning to recognize the difference. When spiritual dryness is from God, it will ultimately draw you closer, producing humility and dependence. When it is from the enemy, it will push you further away, producing despair and unbelief. That is why Paul urged believers not to be ignorant of Satan's devices (2 Corinthians 2:11), but also to remember that God *"is faithful, who will*

Spiritual Warfare: Building Your Battle Plan

not suffer you to be tempted above that ye are able" (1 Corinthians 10:13).

Recognition

Recognizing a spiritual attack on your walk with God takes humility and prayer. You must be willing to ask, *"Is this a season where God is testing and stretching my faith, or is the enemy trying to pull me away from Him?"*

Both can initially feel the same, but there is a way to distinguish between them. When God allows silence, His purpose is to mature your faith. He is teaching you to trust Him beyond feelings, to *"walk by faith, not by sight"* (2 Corinthians 5:7), and to endure so *that "the trying of your faith worketh patience"* (James 1:3). But when the enemy twists that silence, his purpose is the opposite. His purpose is to plant lies in your heart: *"God has abandoned you," "your prayers don't matter," "you are unloved."*

The key is to notice the direction the silence takes you. If it pushes you to trust more in God and deepen your faith, it is likely a season of growth. But if it drives you into despair, bitterness, or isolation, it may be the enemy at work.

This is one of Satan's most effective weapons. If he convinces you that God has turned away, he can tempt you to stop praying. If he persuades you that your words are unheard, he can push you to close your Bible. If he whispers that you are unloved, he can harden your heart. His goal is to drive a wedge into your fellowship with God (1 John 1:7).

God has not left you. The silence does not mean His absence. Feelings rise and fall, but His promise still stands (Hebrews 13:5). Even when emotions insist He is far away, His Word declares He is near.

**Spiritual attacks aim at
your fellowship with God.**

Chapter 2: Recognizing the Attack

A Final Word on Recognition

Not every hardship is a spiritual attack. Sometimes what we face is simply the reality of living in a fallen world. Bodies grow weak, minds grow tired, and life brings sorrow. That does not always mean Satan is striking.

Other times, the real issue is our own sin. Sin will keep you from prayer. Sin will close your Bible. Sin will drive you from church. As Scripture says, *"Every man is tempted, when he is drawn away of his own lust, and enticed"* (James 1:14). Many Christians blame the devil for what is really the fruit of their own flesh.

Still at other times, the problem is just poor choices. Overspending leads to debt, which is not always an attack, but poor stewardship. Neglecting your health may bring sickness, not because of Satan, but because of neglect. Staying up all night and then finding you cannot pray in the morning is not spiritual warfare. It is simply a lack of discipline. Not every hardship is from the enemy. Rather, it is the result of our own decisions.

However, if you dismiss every repeated struggle as *"just life,"* you risk missing the times when the enemy is truly at work.

You must learn to recognize and discern. This means avoiding both extremes, not superstition that sees the devil in every shadow, but also not blindness that ignores his attacks. It means asking honestly: Is this an attack? Is this chastening? Or is this the fruit of my own decisions?

Stand firm in the truth,
and you will not fall.

So let me remind you again: not every hardship is an attack. But if trials keep coming again and again, if the timing always seems to follow spiritual victories, and if the pressure is clearly aimed at weakening your faith, do not shrug it off. Learn to recognize the difference, and you will know how to fight the right battle.

The enemy is real, but so is your Defender. The devil strikes, but he is not sovereign. God sets the limits, as He did with Job, and He promises that *"God is faithful, who will not suffer you to be tempted above that ye are able"* (1 Corinthians 10:13). And no matter how fierce the attack, His grace will not fail you.

2

BUILD YOUR BATTLE PLAN

RECOGNIZE THE ATTACK

Before a soldier can fight, he must know exactly who, or what, he's up against. If you misidentify the enemy, you will start blaming everything else. Your spouse becomes the target. Your boss becomes the villain. Your circumstances feel like the whole problem. Or you collapse inward and drown in your own emotions. All the while, the real enemy slips around unnoticed. That's why it is important to recognize the battle.

This *Battle Plan* isn't about jumping into the fight yet. That time is coming soon enough. Right now, the goal is to sharpen your discernment. This is where you begin learning to tell the difference between:

- ordinary struggles that come with life in a fallen world
- consequences of your own choices
- chastening from the Lord
- and the distinct marks of spiritual attack

These pages are where you begin mapping your own battleground. Recognizing what's really going on isn't the knockout blow, Recognizing what's really going on isn't the knockout blow, but it keeps you from wasting all your energy swinging at shadows, or worse, striking the wrong target.

Step 1: Pray for Discernment

Ask God for wisdom to see clearly, and humility to be honest.

How to do it:

1. Find a quiet place to pray.
2. Read these verses slowly as part of your prayer:

   "If any of you lack wisdom, let him ask of God, that giveth to all men liberally, and upbraideth not; and it shall be given him." (James 1:5)

   "Search me, O God, and know my heart: try me, and know my thoughts: And see if there be any wicked way in me, and lead me in the way everlasting." (Psalm 139:23–24)

3. Pray through these four discernment requests:

   - Life: *"Father, show me what is simply the sorrow of a fallen world."*

   - Choices: *"Show me if my own decisions have brought this on and give me humility to repent."*

   - Chastening: *"If You are correcting me, help me to hear and to be trained by it."*

   - Attack: *"If the enemy is attacking, help me recognize it quickly without fear."*

Step 2: Identify Your Common Battlegrounds

Job's story shows that attacks can come in waves. Scripture and life also show that pressure often repeats in familiar places. Recognition begins when patterns become visible.

How to do it:

1. Look back over the last 6–12 months. Where have the struggles come in clusters, waves, or at unusual times?

2. Check the battleground(s) where you have felt the most pressure.

   ☐ Physical (health, strength, exhaustion).
   ☐ Emotional (fear, discouragement, anger, sudden sadness).
   ☐ Financial (losses, sudden expenses, debts).
   ☐ Relational (conflict, betrayal, division, isolation).
   ☐ Mental (racing thoughts, confusion, lies, distraction).
   ☐ Spiritual (difficulty praying, reading the Bible, sense of God's absence).

3. Pause and answer these two questions in writing:

   Did these struggles happen all at once, or come in waves?

   Did it intensify around spiritual obedience or spiritual growth?

4. Briefly describe why you checked any of these.

   Physical:

   Emotional:

   Financial:

   Relational:

   Mental:

   Spiritual:

Step 3: Record One Clear Experience

Put into words what you have faced so that you can begin to recognize the difference between ordinary hardship and a spiritual attack. Writing it down exposes the pattern.

How to do it:

1. Choose one or two battlegrounds you checked in **Step 2.**

2. Write a specific example from your life where you have felt pressure. Keep it simple, but honest.

   What happened?

   When did it happen?

   Did it come suddenly, or in a wave of troubles?

What spiritual decision did you make around that time (if any)?

How did you respond at that time?

3. Now compare your experience to Job's pattern in Job 1:13–19.
   - Did this come at an unusual time, after a step of obedience?
   - Did it feel designed to weaken your trust in God?
   - Do you see a *"while one was yet speaking"* pattern where problems come in waves?

   Write your reflection here:

Step 4: Discern the Source

This chapter warns against misdiagnosis. Not every hardship is a spiritual attack, and not every hardship is merely *"life."* Discernment requires honest questions.

After reviewing what you wrote in **Step 3**, answer the following:

1. **Life in a fallen world:** Could this simply be the normal pain of living in a broken world (illness, loss, inconvenience)?

2. **My own choices:** Did I create this problem by my own actions, neglect, or sin?

3. **God's chastening:** Could this be the Lord's correction, meant to draw me back? (Hebrews 12:6)

4. **Satan's attack:** Does the timing, intensity, and repetition suggest the enemy's hand—especially striking after spiritual victory or obedience?

When you finish, look back at your answers. If you see a pattern of repeated blows, unusual timing, and pressure aimed at your faith, you may be facing a spiritual attack.

Step 5: Practice Recognition This Week

Recognition becomes useful when it becomes a habit. This week is not about fixing everything. It is about refusing to misdiagnose the battle.

How to do it:

1. Each time pressure rises this week, stop and ask:
   - Is this just life in a fallen world?
   - Is this connected to my own choices?
   - Is this God's correction?
   - Or is this the spiritual attack?

2. When unsure, pray: *"Lord, give me wisdom to discern. Do not let me fight the wrong enemy."*

3. Write one way you will put recognition into practice this week. (Example: pausing before speaking in conflict, praying before reacting to discouragement, or asking God for wisdom when finances tighten).

   My step of recognition this week:

3

RESPONDING TO THE ATTACK

*When darkness advances,
worship becomes your weapon.*

You've taken the first big step. You've learned to recognize the attack. You've seen the signs in your body, emotions, finances, relationships, mind, and spirit. That awareness is powerful. It pulls back the curtain and shows you the real enemy at work.

But here's the truth I want to speak straight to you: recognition alone doesn't win the battle. It's the starting point, not the finish line. You can spot every move the enemy makes, quote verses about his schemes, even teach others how he works, and still lose ground if recognition never turns into obedient response.

The enemy wants you aware but inactive. He's happy if you know it's him, as long as you don't do anything about it. That's why this chapter is so important.

God doesn't want you just informed. He wants you standing strong, resisting the devil in His power. *"Submit yourselves therefore to God.*

Resist the devil, and he will flee from you" (James 4:7). That's the strategy. Submit first. Resist second. When you do both, the enemy

Spiritual Warfare: Building Your Battle Plan

has to flee.

I've counseled believers who could name every attack but still felt defeated. They knew it was spiritual. They could see the patterns. But they reacted in the flesh, tried harder, prayed louder, felt guilty when it didn't stop. Response isn't about more effort. It's about right obedience.

**Recognition is the call to arms.
Response is the fight.**

The Wrong Ways to Respond

Before we look at the right way, let's be honest about the wrong ways. Because most of us start here.

I've counseled believers who could name every attack but still felt defeated. They knew it was spiritual. They could see the patterns clear as day. But when the pressure hit, they reacted in the flesh. They tried harder, prayed louder, pushed themselves to *"have more faith,"* and then felt guilty when it didn't stop the attack. They thought if they just put in more effort, God would finally move. But response isn't about more effort. It's about right obedience.

That's the trap. You see the enemy coming, but you fight him the wrong way. You swing with your own strength instead of standing in His. And the enemy loves it, because flesh can't win a spiritual fight.

I've seen good people fall into this. A brother facing doubt would read extra chapters, pray extra hours, promise God he'd do better. But the doubt stayed. A sister under emotional attack would journal more, listen to more sermons, try to *"feel"* victory. But the heaviness lingered. They weren't lazy. They were sincere. But sincerity without the right response just leaves you tired.

Wrong responses waste your strength. They leave you worn out while the enemy gains ground.

Job: Caught in the Middle of a Spiritual Attack

When we left Job, he was sitting in ashes, stripped of his wealth, his children, and his health. Everything collapsed in waves. No pause. No

Chapter 3: Responding to the Attack

explanation. Just loss after loss. Yet in that devastation, Job made one choice that changed everything. He responded with humble worship before God. *"Then Job arose, and rent his mantle, and shaved his head, and fell down upon the ground, and worshipped"* (Job 1:20).

That verse is the turning point of Job's story. When he recognized that he was under spiritual attack, he chose to worship God. He didn't understand the why, but he knew the Who, the Lord Himself. He ran to God instead of away from Him.

Job's first act after loss was not to fight back, question why, or retreat. It was to bow. That's what it means to worship. That's where victory begins. When your first response to spiritual attack is worship, you've already robbed the enemy of his foothold. Job's worship closed every door the enemy could use.

"In all this Job sinned not, nor charged God foolishly" (Job 1:22). Satan's goal was never about Job's suffering. It was Job's surrender to doubt. He said, *"Doth Job fear God for nought?"* seeking to prove that faith would fail when tested (Job 1:9–11). But when Job refused to curse God, he turned Satan's weapon back on himself.

That's the same choice you face in every spiritual attack. The enemy cannot force you to doubt. He can only tempt you. Whether it's sickness, fear, loss, or confusion, the battle is decided in that moment of choice: Will you react in the flesh, or respond in faith?

Job's worship didn't stop the pain.
It stopped the enemy's plan.

Recognition is a Call, not a Conclusion

It's not enough to say, *"I know what's happening."* The next step is, *"Now I know what to do."* Awareness without obedience is like spotting the enemy at the gate and leaving the door unlocked. You may understand the danger, but you've done nothing to stop it.

When Paul wrote to the Corinthians, he warned, *"Lest Satan should get an advantage of us: for we are not ignorant of his devices"* (2 Corinthians 2:11). That word *"devices"* means his plans or strategies. The phrase *"get an advantage"* means to outwit or gain the upper hand. Satan wins when knowledge never becomes action.

Spiritual Warfare: Building Your Battle Plan

That's why the Lord doesn't just want you informed; He wants you armed. *"Take unto you the whole armour of God, that ye may be able to withstand in the evil day"* (Ephesians 6:13). Recognition identifies the fight. Response engages it.

The enemy counts on hesitation. He hopes you'll sit frozen in fear or stay busy in self-effort. The moment you choose to act, to pray, to stand on Scripture, to resist, you move from defense to offense. That is, from reaction to action. The Spirit of God within you strengthens and enables you, and the same power that raised Christ from the dead works in you and through you as you obey in faith (Ephesians 1:19–20; Philippians 2:13).

That's the turning point of every battle.

You can't stop the enemy from attacking, but you can choose how you'll respond.

Faith, Not Flesh

Every believer must come to this truth: the way you respond to the attack will shape what God can do through your battle. When the devil strikes, your flesh wants to fix it yourself, to fight, or to flee. But none of those work in spiritual warfare.

The flesh wants to fix—to argue, reason, or manipulate.
The flesh wants to fight—to lash out in anger or self-defense.
The flesh wants to flee—to escape, numb, or run from the pain.

But the Spirit calls you to faith, to run to God, not from Him. Faith doesn't deny the attack. It declares that God is greater than the battle.

Remember what Jesus said when Peter tried to protect Him from the cross: *"Get thee behind me, Satan: thou art an offence unto me: for thou savourest not the things that be of God, but those that be of men"* (Matthew 16:23). Peter's words sounded loyal, but they were rooted in human reasoning. Jesus recognized the source behind them, and He responded immediately.

That's the first step of victory: call the attack for what it is. Don't argue with it. Don't analyze it. Don't entertain it. Just name it, resist

Chapter 3: Responding to the Attack

it, and replace it with truth. That's what we'll learn in the pages ahead, five clear, biblical ways to respond when the enemy begins to attack.

However, before we move into those steps, you must first understand that you cannot fight a spiritual battle with *natural* weapons. Prayer, Scripture, and obedience are not your fallback options; they are the only weapons that work.

So when awareness turns to action, the tide begins to turn. The battle may not end immediately, but the outcome is already written: *"But thanks be to God, which giveth us the victory through our Lord Jesus Christ"* (1 Corinthians 15:57).

Faith, not flesh, is the way forward.

Responding to The Attack

Step 1: Call It What It Is

When Jesus turned to Peter and said, *"Get thee behind me, Satan"* (Matthew 16:23), He wasn't calling Peter the devil; He was naming the source behind the words. Peter's concern sounded compassionate, *"Be it far from thee, Lord,"* but the subtle lie underneath was deadly: avoid the cross. That's how the enemy operates. He hides behind natural voices, logical reasoning, or emotional persuasion.

That's why one of the first steps to victory is to call the attack what it really is.

Too many believers lose strength because they refuse to name the battle. They label it as *"just bad luck," "just stress,"* or *"just life."* But you cannot fight what you refuse to identify. Recognition without naming it leaves the enemy's disguise intact.

When temptation whispers, *"No one will notice,"* call it what it is, a lie from the pit of hell. When discouragement tells you, *"God has forgotten you,"* call it what it is, a dart from the enemy. When confusion clouds your mind, say it out loud: *"This is not from God!"* For the Bible says, *"for God is not the author of confusion"* (1

Spiritual Warfare: Building Your Battle Plan

Corinthians 14:33).

Calling it what it is doesn't mean shouting into the air; it means aligning your thoughts with truth. It's spiritual clarity. Every soldier in combat must first identify the target. The enemy's success depends on deception, on his ability to operate unnoticed. The moment you recognize the attack and name it, you strip away his camouflage.

In my own life, there have been seasons when fear and anxiety tried to take hold. I recall one night in particular when my heart began racing for no apparent reason. It felt physical, but I knew in my spirit it was more than that. I stopped and said, *"Lord, this isn't from You."* That prayer was short, but it marked a shift. The fear didn't vanish instantly, but its hold lost power as God's truth took authority over it. Why? Because I stopped treating it like a random feeling and called it what it was, an attack against peace.

Calling it what it is exposes the lie and brings light.

Step 2: Run to God, Not from Him

Every attack carries a temptation to withdraw. Fear says, *"Hide."* Shame says, *"Stay away."* Pride says, *"Handle it yourself."* Yet each of those responses pulls you further from your only source of help. When pressure comes, the flesh runs from God, but faith runs to Him.

Psalm 145:18 declares, *"The LORD is nigh unto all them that call upon him, to all that call upon him in truth."* The Lord does not stand distant, waiting for you to earn His attention. He draws near the very moment you call out to Him in sincerity. The enemy knows this. That's why he works hardest to isolate you in silence. If he can make you feel unworthy to pray, he can keep you unarmed. Prayer is not for the perfect; it's for the desperate and the dependent.

When Job sat in ashes, scraping his boils, he still spoke to God. When David sinned, he didn't hide forever. He cried, *"Have mercy upon me, O God"* (Psalm 51:1). When Peter sank beneath the waves, he shouted, *"Lord, save me!"* (Matthew 14:30). Each of those prayers was short, yet every one brought deliverance.

Chapter 3: Responding to the Attack

Running to God doesn't mean feeling strong. It means admitting you aren't. The moment you turn toward Him in prayer, you've already resisted the enemy's plan. I've counseled believers who, under attack, said, *"I don't feel like praying."* My answer is always the same: <u>pray anyway</u>. Prayer isn't a feeling. it's an act of faith, a Spirit-led movement of the heart toward God (Romans 8:26–27; Hebrews 11:6). You don't wait for peace to pray. You pray until peace comes.

The devil wants you silent because silence feels safe to the natural self, but deadly to the spirit. Every whispered prayer of faith is a declaration of war. Psalm 18:6 says, *"In my distress I called upon the LORD, and cried unto my God: he heard my voice out of his temple, and my cry came before him, even into his ears."* Even in distress, God hears. Especially in distress, He listens.

When you run to Him, you're not escaping reality. You're running into the only safe place left standing. *"The name of the LORD is a strong tower: the righteous runneth into it, and is safe"* (Proverbs 18:10).

**Running to God
is the safest move in battle.**

Step 3: Get Into the Word Immediately

When the enemy attacks, emotions scream and thoughts scatter. In that moment, feelings can't be trusted, but the Word of God stands firm. *"For the word of God is quick, and powerful, and sharper than any twoedged sword"* (Hebrews 4:12). The Word is not just information. It is a living weapon of truth.

Every time Jesus was tempted in the wilderness, He answered, *"It is written"* (Matthew 4). He didn't debate, reason, or panic. He wielded Scripture. The Word became both His defense and His weapon of victory. The same strategy works today. The moment you recognize an attack, go straight to the Word of God. Don't wait until Sunday. Don't rely on memory alone. Open your Bible and anchor your mind in what God has already said.

Spiritual Warfare: Building Your Battle Plan

I have experienced this firsthand. Not long ago, our church came under a spiritual attack. It was one of the most hurtful seasons of my ministry. At first, I didn't even recognize it as a spiritual attack. But once I did, I gathered our staff and we called it for what it was. We prayed, and then we turned together to the book of Philippians. As we walked through that entire book, God spoke to us in specific ways. He revealed what was happening, and even showed us things that were about to happen before they came to pass. In doing so, He prepared us for the battle ahead. It was amazing to hear God speak directly to us and strengthen us through His Word during that time.

That's what the Word of God does. It speaks with living power into present battles. The same Scriptures that sustained us will sustain you. When fear rises, when confusion clouds your mind, when strength seems gone, there is always a word from God waiting to meet you.

In times of fear, turn to Psalm 27.
In times of confusion, turn to James 1.
In times of weakness, turn to Isaiah 40.
In times of spiritual dryness, turn to Psalm 63.

When you immerse yourself in the Word, you're not escaping the battle; you're stepping into God's armory, the place where His weapons of truth are kept. *"Thy word is a lamp unto my feet, and a light unto my path"* (Psalm 119:105). Light does two things: it exposes danger and reveals direction. That's exactly what the Word does when you're under fire.

Many believers lose ground because they wait until the crisis peaks before opening their Bible. The Word is not a last resort. It is your first line of defense. Make it personal. Write down verses that speak directly to your struggle. Keep them where you can see them: on your phone, your dashboard, and your mirror. The more the Word fills your mind, the less room there is for the enemy's lies.

**The Word spoken in faith
turns defense into advance.**

Chapter 3: Responding to the Attack

Step 4: Quote Scripture Out Loud

This is where many believers stop short. They read the Word silently but never declare it. Yet throughout Scripture, the power of spoken truth is unmistakable. When Jesus faced the devil in the wilderness, He didn't merely think the Word. He spoke it: *"It is written..."* (Matthew 4:4, 7, 10). Each time, the spoken Word silenced Satan.

Speaking Scripture aloud is not a ritual or superstition. It is an act of submission. You are agreeing with God out loud. You are letting your own ears hear what your heart believes. *"So then, faith cometh by hearing, and hearing by the word of God"* (Romans 10:17). Hearing truth strengthens faith, and faith breaks fear.

When you speak God's Word, two things happen: you remind your own soul what is true, and you resist the devil with the authority of Scripture. When you submit to God in obedience, the enemy has no choice but to retreat. (James 4:7). That's not theory. It's a promise. The enemy doesn't flee because of your tone or volume, but because of the authority behind the Word you speak.

There have been times in ministry when discouragement hit hard and unexpectedly. In those moments, I have stood alone in my office and spoken Scripture aloud, not shouting, but declaring: *"The LORD is my light and my salvation; whom shall I fear?"* (Psalm 27:1). Each time, peace began to push back the oppression. That is how spiritual warfare works: truth spoken in faith drives back lies whispered in fear.

You cannot outthink him, but you can overcome him with truth. Every *"It is written"* cuts deeper than any accusation he throws your way. So when the attack comes, open your Bible and open your mouth. Speak God's promises over your fear, your family, your mind, and your heart. Let the Word fill the space around you, your home, your workplace, and your thoughts, for the devil cannot stand against the authority of God's Word when it is declared in faith.

**You cannot argue with the devil,
but you can answer him with Scripture.**

Spiritual Warfare: Building Your Battle Plan

Step 5: Seek Help, Don't Fight Alone

One of the enemy's oldest tricks is isolation. He wants you to believe no one will understand, no one will care, and no one can help. But that's a lie designed to keep you alone and defenseless. *"Two are better than one; because they have a good reward for their labour. For if they fall, the one will lift up his fellow"* (Ecclesiastes 4:9–10). Every soldier in battle needs a comrade, and every believer in warfare needs a brother or sister in Christ who will stand beside them.

When you're under attack, pride whispers, *"You can handle it yourself."* But independence is not true strength. It's self-reliance disguised as strength. God designed His people for fellowship. When Moses' arms grew weary on the mountain, Aaron and Hur held them up, and the battle below was won (Exodus 17:12). That's the power of partnership in spiritual warfare.

Sometimes victory doesn't come through another sermon. It comes through another believer praying with you. Sometimes what you need most is not advice but companionship, someone's steady presence that reminds you you're not alone. This is why church matters. The local church isn't just a place to attend. It is the army God assembled for your protection. When you isolate yourself, you walk away from your reinforcements.

"Not forsaking the assembling of ourselves together, but exhorting one another" (Hebrews 10:25). The word *"exhorting"* means encouraging and strengthening. That's what happens when believers gather. The Spirit of God works through the fellowship of the saints to build courage and renew resolve (Philippians 2:1–2; Acts 2:42).

> **You're not meant to fight alone.**
> **God gave you the church for a reason.**

In my own ministry, I have seen countless times when a weary believer found renewed strength simply by sharing their battle with someone godly. It wasn't counseling techniques or deep insight. It was the simple power of prayer and presence. If you're in a fight, don't face it alone. Find a trusted Christian who knows the Word and walks with

Chapter 3: Responding to the Attack

God. Ask them to pray with you and hold you accountable. That one humble step can close the door of isolation and open the door of victory.

Don't Forget the Good News

The enemy's attack and pressure are real, but God's presence is greater. Every attack in Scripture eventually reveals that truth. The devil strikes to destroy, but God uses even the enemy's weapons to strengthen His people. As Joseph declared, *"But as for you, ye thought evil against me; but God meant it unto good"* (Genesis 50:20).

When Job's trial reached its darkest hour, when the ashes had cooled and the tears had dried, Scripture says, *"And the LORD turned the captivity of Job, when he prayed for his friends: also the LORD gave Job twice as much as he had before"* (Job 42:10). Notice the order: Job's victory didn't come when he proved his strength, but when he surrendered his pride. His response wasn't revenge. It was prayer. He prayed for his friends who had accused and misunderstood him, and in that act of humble obedience, God restored him.

That is the heartbeat of this chapter. Victory doesn't begin when the pain ends; it begins when you respond in faith. *"The LORD is my rock, and my fortress, and my deliverer; my God, my strength, in whom I will trust"* (Psalm 18:2). That verse isn't theory. It's testimony. David wrote it after being chased, betrayed, and hunted. But he learned something powerful: the same God who allows the test also sets its limits and supplies the strength.

The believer's story is not one of defeat but of endurance. When you respond in faith, the battle may still rage, but the victory, already secured by Christ's finished work, is simply claimed by faith. As Paul wrote, victory belongs to us through our Lord Jesus Christ (1 Corinthians 15:57).

You are not forsaken or powerless. The same Spirit that raised Jesus from the dead dwells in you (Romans 8:11). The same Word that silenced Satan in the wilderness is in your hands. The same spiritual armor that Paul described in Ephesians 6 still fits today.

That means no matter what comes, sickness, fear, loss, temptation, or confusion, you have not been left defenseless. You have

Spiritual Warfare: Building Your Battle Plan

been equipped. When you pray, God hears. When you speak God's Word in faith and submission, darkness trembles at its authority (James 4:7; Ephesians 6:17). When you obey, the devil loses ground in your life. When you worship in the middle of pain, you declare whose side you're on and whose power you trust.

The Christian life isn't about avoiding battles. It's about overcoming them through Christ. Jesus Himself promised, *"In the world ye shall have tribulation: but be of good cheer; I have overcome the world"* (John 16:33). That victory is not distant or theoretical. It's personal and present.

You are not fighting for victory.
You are fighting from victory.

Closing Challenge: Will You Stand?

Every reader must answer this question: when the next attack comes, will you stand?

Standing doesn't mean feeling fearless. It means refusing to bow to fear. It means that when the blows come, your heart still declares, *"Though he slay me, yet will I trust in him"* (Job 13:15). When temptation whispers, your lips still answer, *"It is written."* And when the storm rages, you do not let go of your faith. The God who gave you faith is the One who holds you fast (1 Peter 1:5; Philippians 1:6; Jude 1:24).

"And having done all, to stand" (Ephesians 6:13). That's not passive. It's a posture of victory. Standing means you've already resisted, you've already trusted, and you're not giving ground back.

That's the decision every believer must make long before the battle begins. The time to decide to stand is now, in quiet moments of devotion, in times of peace, in the strength of the Lord.

So I ask again: will you stand? If your answer is yes, then let's take the next step and make it practical.

3

BUILD YOUR BATTLE PLAN

RESPOND THE ATTACK

You already learned how to recognize the battle. But seeing the fight is not the same as reacting to it. What you do next matters just as much as recognizing the attack.

Most of the time, we don't lose our footing because the enemy stays hidden. We lost it because we responded incorrectly. Many believers correctly identify the attack, then answer it in their own strength. They react instead of obeying. They lash out emotionally, shut down in silence, or try to push through the pressure with sheer willpower.

That is why this *Battle Plan* is not about trying harder. Real strength is not found in intense reaction, but in simple obedience. When your response lines up with God's Word and His Spirit, your responsibility shifts. The outcome no longer rests on you. It rests on Him. That is where obedience does its work, and that is where real victory is found.

Purpose of This Battle Plan

This plan is designed to help you:
- Cut off flesh-driven reactions before they take control.
- Replace gut instincts with faithful obedience.
- Respond in ways that weaken the enemy.
- Learn habits that will equip you until we get to the final, long-term *Battle Plan* at the end of this book.

Step 1: Call Out the Attack

Once you have recognized the situation as a spiritual attack, the first response is not emotion, explanation, or self-correction. The first response is <u>refusal of ownership.</u>

Many believers recognize the attack correctly, then immediately take responsibility for it. They say, *"This is just me," "I'm failing again,"* or *"I need to fix this."* In doing so, they accept the pressure as personal instead of responding spiritually.

Jesus immediately named the source and shut it down: *"Get thee behind me, Satan"* (Matthew 16:23).

How to do it?

1. Acknowledge the attack clearly.
   You already discerned the attack. (See Chapter 2)

2. Give credit where credit is due.
   Silently or aloud, say: "Get behind me Satan!"

3. Do not take credit for the enemy's attack.
   Do not say: "It's me," "It's my fault," or "I'm the problem."

If you have rightly identified this as a spiritual attack, it is dangerous to take responsibility for it. When you take credit for what the enemy is doing, you shift the battle into the flesh. When you respond correctly, you keep the fight where it belongs.

Now It's Your Turn:

This is where the rubber meets the road. No more letting the enemy operate in the shadows. You're going to name this attack out loud and in writing. Take your time. Answer these honestly and specifically.

1. What specifically made you identify this situation as a spiritual attack and not merely stress, habit, or circumstance?

2. What words or thoughts have you been using, maybe without even realizing it, that take ownership of this attack? (Examples: *"This is just me," "I always mess this up," "I'm failing again."*)

3. Write the phrase you will use when this attack returns: (Example: *"Get behind me, Satan."*)

Step 2: Turn to God Immediately

Once you have called out the attack and told Satan to *"get behind you,"* do not pause. Your next step is to turn to God immediately.

Every spiritual attack creates momentum. If that momentum is not redirected, it will pull you toward isolation, self-effort, or emotional reaction. Turning to God right away is an act of submission. It is choosing to rely on Him instead of remaining in your own strength.

How you do it?

1. **Turn your attention to God.**
   Deliberately focus on who He is.
   Call to mind His character, His authority, His power.
   Bring your thoughts back under His truth.

2. **Confess where needed.**
   Confess sin.
   Do not justify it. Do not hide it.
   Repentance matters before moving forward.

3. **Surrender the situation.**
   "Lord, I submit this to You."
   "Lord, I need Your help right now."
   "Lord, I trust You here."

4. **Depend on Him.**
   Tell him what is happening.
   Stay engaged with Him.
   Refuse to disconnect or pull away.

5. **Do not try to fix the situation yet.**
   This is not the problem-solving step.
   Be still. Listen.

6. **Thank Him in advance.**
   Acknowledge His faithfulness.
   Trust He will answer.

Now It's Your Turn:

This is where you put it into practice. No more reading about it, time to make it yours. Be honest. Write these out. This is between you and the Lord, and it's how you start building the habit of responding right when the pressure hits.

1. Where do you usually turn first when pressure hits? *(Distraction, problem-solving, withdrawal, emotion, self-effort.)*

2. Write one sentence of submission you will use immediately when the attack starts. (Example: *"Lord, I submit this moment to You. I need Your help now."*)

3. Is there any known sin, resistance, or avoidance that needs to be confessed before moving forward? *Write it down. No explanation.*

4. Write one sentence expressing dependence on God instead of control. (Example: *"Father, I can't fix this and I won't try—I'm depending on You to carry it."*)

5. Write one way you will intentionally pause instead of taking control when this attack begins. (*"I will stop everything and pray out loud before I say or do anything else."*)

Step 3: Anchor Yourself in the Word

You've turned to God. You've submitted, confessed, surrendered, and poured it all out to Him. But don't stop there. The next move is to anchor yourself in His Word.

Where to Start?

Begin with passages that establish perspective, not explanation.

- **Job** — when the battle feels overwhelming or unfair.
- **Psalms** — when emotions are loud and unstable.
- **Proverbs** — when clarity and restraint are needed.

These books are not chosen for information, but for alignment.

How to do it?

1. **Choose one book.**
   Do not rotate. Stay anchored.

2. **Read slowly and in order.**
   Start at the beginning of that book.
   No skipping. No rushing.

3. **Do not analyze or outline.**
   This isn't Bible study time. This is grounding time.
   Let the Word wash over you without trying to dissect it.

4. **Read until your thoughts settle.**
   You're not looking for every question to get answered. You're looking for steadiness. Read until the chaos in your head quiets down even a little.

The Word will not always stop the attack immediately, but it will remove confusion. Confusion is one of the enemy's favorite weapons, and anchoring yourself in Scripture takes it out of his hands.

Now It's Your Turn:

This is personal now. No more theory. You're locking in how you'll anchor yourself in the Word when the attack hits. Choose carefully, commit clearly, and write it down. This becomes your lifeline.

1. Which book will you anchor in during this season?
   Choice one:
   - ☐ *Job*
   - ☐ *Psalms*
   - ☐ *Proverbs*

2. Why did you choose this book?

3. Commit to one specific reading rhythm (be realistic):
   - ☐ _____ *chapters per day.*
   - ☐ _____ *minutes/ hours per day.*
   - ☐ *Reading until my thoughts settle.*

4. Write one sentence reminding yourself why this step matters when the pressure remains.

Step 4: Speak Truth Aloud

You've anchored yourself in the Word. But it has to come out. It has to move into the moment. This step isn't symbolic or optional. It's functional. Speaking God's truth out loud does something nothing else can: it cuts through lies, it steadies your racing mind, and it locks in your submission to Him.

How to do it?

1. **Choose one verse from your reading.**
   Don't go hunting for the "perfect" one.
   Just take the one that stood out.

2. **Read it aloud slowly.**
   Let your own ears hear what God has said.

3. **Repeat it if needed.**
   Say it again. And again if the pressure is still loud.
   This is not performance. It is reinforcement.

4. **Let Scripture, not emotion, set the tone.**
   You're not venting. You're agreeing with God out loud.
   You're saying, *"Yes, Lord. This is true. I stand on this."*

What this actually does:

- It breaks mental attacks the enemy places in your head.
- It reinforces truth changing how you think and feel.
- It resists the enemy without giving him.

Faith grows by hearing, *"and hearing by the word of God"* (Romans 10:17). And right now, in the heat of the attack, you need your faith stronger than ever.

Now It's Your Turn:

This step matters because it moves truth off the page and into the fight. When Scripture comes out of your mouth, it does not remain theoretical. It becomes a weapon God has placed in your hands.

Write these out now. Be specific. Do not generalize. This is your plan for the next moment the pressure returns.

1. Write the verse you will speak aloud when this attack begins.

2. Where will you speak it?
   - ☐ Alone in the car
   - ☐ Out loud in prayer
   - ☐ In the middle of anxiety or racing thoughts
   - ☐ Before sleep
   - ☐ In the face of temptation
   - ☐ Other: _____

3. Write one sentence describing what usually happens in your mind before you speak Scripture.

4. Write one sentence describing what usually happens in your mind *after* you speak Scripture.

Step 5: Stay Connected and Hold the Line

You've done the hard work. You've recognized the attack, turned to God, anchored in His Word, spoken truth out loud. Now the enemy will try his favorite follow-up move: get you to isolate. That's when attacks often ramp up, because isolation hands him the ground you just took back.

This step is about refusing to retreat after the initial stand. It's not about fixing the problem yet. It's about not giving one inch back to the enemy.

How to do it?

1. **Do not withdraw.**
   Keep praying. Keep reading. Keep showing up.

2. **Go to church.**
   Do not separate yourself from the place God uses for strength, accountability, and encouragement.

3. **Resist the urge to reassess constantly.**
   You do not need to re-analyze the attack every day. You have already identified it and responded.

4. **End each day with surrender, not evaluation.**
   The question is not "Did it stop?"
   The question is "Did I obey?"

What This Does:

- It blocks isolation before it starts.
- It guards against discouragement.
- It keeps you obedience steady while God works.

Holding the line isn't wasting time. It's disciplined faith. It's choosing, day after day, to stay connected and stand exactly where God has placed you until He moves the battle or moves you.

Now It's Your Turn:

This is where many battles are quietly lost, not because the enemy overpowers, but because the pressure lingers and the whisper of doubts makes it seem easier to give up.

1. What is your first instinct during prolonged attack?
    ☐ Withdraw
    ☐ Isolate
    ☐ Reassess constantly
    ☐ Stay steady

2. Write one decision you are making now to remain connected to your church during this season.

3. Name one trusted believer you will not isolate from during this battle.

4. Write one sentence you will use to remind yourself that obedience matters more than relief.

5. Complete this sentence:
    "Even if the attack continues, I will remain _____
    _____."

4

PREVENTING THE ATTACK

The easiest battle to win is the one the enemy never gets to fight.

You've learned how to recognize the attack and how to respond when it comes. But a wise soldier doesn't just wait for the next blow. He guards the gates before the enemy ever reaches them. Recognition and resistance are vital, but prevention keeps the battle from moving inside. That's the goal of this chapter: to learn how to close the doors the devil loves to use.

It was late at night when a family in a quiet neighborhood heard a faint sound in their living room. The front door was locked. The windows were closed. Everything looked secure. But earlier that evening, they had stepped outside and left a side door cracked open, just a few inches. That was all it took for an intruder to slip in unnoticed. The safest place in the world suddenly felt like the most dangerous.

That's how the devil works. He rarely kicks the door down. He waits for an opening. If you leave even the smallest crack, an unchecked attitude, a secret thought, a neglected duty, he will take it. You may think you are safe, but the enemy sees the invitation.

Spiritual Warfare: Building Your Battle Plan

We saw it first in Eden. *"Yea, hath God said...?"* (Genesis 3:1). One small question opened the door to doubt, and doubt opened the door to sin. The peace of paradise was shattered because the door was left unguarded. Paul warned believers the same way: *"Neither give place to the devil"* (Ephesians 4:27). To give place means to give him room, a foothold, a starting point. He doesn't need control. He only needs your cooperation, the smallest agreement with his deception. The moment you grant him that space, he begins to build a stronghold.

The Holy Spirit, however, is always alert to protect you. He stirs the conscience, presses on the heart, and quietly says, *"That needs to be made right."* If you ignore His voice, the door stays cracked. If you obey it, the door shuts tight.

Satan cannot force his way into the life of a child of God. He must be given entry. Every temptation he offers is an invitation, and every invitation requires permission. That is why small compromises matter so deeply. A thought left unchallenged becomes a foothold. A foothold grows into a habit. A habit hardens into bondage. The Holy Spirit warns early. He doesn't wait until the house is burning. He calls out when the smoke first appears. When you respond to that warning, the fire dies before it spreads. But if you silence His voice, the enemy gains ground inch by inch until you feel trapped and powerless.

The goal of this chapter is simple: recognize those small openings, close them quickly, and keep them shut. This is not about fear, but about faith that acts early. God has given you both the authority through Christ and the help of His Spirit to do it (Luke 10:19; James 4:7; John 14:26).

**Satan cannot let himself in,
you must give him entry.**

The Door of Unconfessed Sin

Sin is like leaving your front door wide open at night, not to your house, but to your soul. You may not see the danger immediately, but the enemy does, and he never ignores an unlocked door.

I once spoke with a man who said, *"Pastor, my prayers feel like they bounce off the ceiling."* He was faithful in church and reading his

Chapter 4: Preventing the Attack

Bible, yet nothing seemed alive. As we talked, the Holy Spirit began pressing on one hidden area of sin, something he had excused for months. He finally admitted it, broke down, and confessed it before the Lord. The very next week, he came back and said, *"It's like the heavens opened again."*

That is exactly what Scripture promises: *"If I regard iniquity in my heart, the Lord will not hear me"* (Psalm 66:18). Hidden sin blocks fellowship and drains spiritual power. David felt it too: *"When I kept silence, my bones waxed old through my roaring all the day long. For day and night thy hand was heavy upon me"* (Psalm 32:3–4).

Unconfessed sin gives Satan leverage, a point of pressure he uses to weaken your walk with God. He uses guilt to whisper, *"You can't pray." "You're a hypocrite."* He uses shame to keep you silent so the door stays open. But the Holy Spirit never condemns. He convicts. He calls you to deal with it now, not later.

Be quick to confess. That's the only way to shut the door fast. Don't wait for Sunday or for a feeling of worthiness. The moment the Spirit brings conviction, agree with God and turn from the sin. *"If we confess our sins, he is faithful and just to forgive us our sins, and to cleanse us from all unrighteousness"* (1 John 1:9).

Confession is not mere admission. It is alignment, seeing sin exactly as God sees it. When you confess and forsake it, the enemy loses his foothold of accusation, and the door swings shut in the strength of Christ's forgiveness (Romans 8:1; Colossians 2:13–15).

Unconfessed sin is an open door.
Confession slams it shut.

The Door of Bitterness and Unforgiveness

Bitterness is one of Satan's favorite doors because it hides behind respectable disguises. We rarely call it *"bitterness."* We call it hurt, or boundaries, or being cautious. We tell ourselves we're protecting our heart, but left alone, that same hurt hardens it.

I once counseled a believer who hadn't spoken to his brother in twelve years. The original disagreement was small, a misunderstanding at a family gathering, but pride kept both men from

Spiritual Warfare: Building Your Battle Plan

yielding. Each thought silence was safer. Yet that silence grew into a wall so thick that even prayer felt empty. The Holy Spirit had been prompting forgiveness for years, but the man resisted, saying, *"It's not my fault."* Meanwhile, joy drained from his life and peace disappeared from his home.

That is the power of bitterness. *"...lest any root of bitterness springing up trouble you, and thereby many be defiled"* (Hebrews 12:15). A root spreads unseen beneath the surface until it poisons everything around it. Bitterness never stays personal. It contaminates marriages, friendships, and even entire churches.

We see the same tragedy in Absalom. Anger over his sister's wrong turned into calculated hatred (2 Samuel 13). What began as righteous anger became murderous rebellion. That story is more than history. It's a warning. That's how the devil works: he takes legitimate pain and twists it into lethal resentment.

Forgive, even if the other person never asks. Forgiveness doesn't excuse their sin. It honors God and releases you to walk in the same grace you've received. *"Let all bitterness, and wrath, and anger... be put away from you... and be ye kind one to another, tenderhearted, forgiving one another, even as God for Christ's sake hath forgiven you"* (Ephesians 4:31–32). Forgiveness isn't weakness. It's warfare, because forgiveness takes back the ground Satan gained through offense. When you forgive, you shut the door that bitterness used to enter.

It is the Holy Spirit who enables that forgiveness. He softens what anger has hardened and reminds you how much you have been forgiven. When you yield to His prompting, grace begins to flow again. If He is stirring your heart about someone right now, do not ignore Him. That gentle conviction is His mercy. Obey it, and peace will return faster than you imagine.

Bitterness opens the door wide.
Forgiveness slams it shut.

Chapter 4: Preventing the Attack

The Door of Distraction

One of the subtlest ways the devil gets in is through distraction. He doesn't always need to tempt you into obvious sin. Sometimes all he needs to do is keep you so busy, so tired, or so entertained that you stop noticing what's happening in your spiritual life. Distraction rarely feels dangerous. It usually feels productive, responsible, or even harmless. Yet over time, it drains your devotion and replaces it with useless noise.

I remember counseling a young lady who told me she felt distant from God. When I asked about her prayer life, her Bible reading, and her church attendance, she admitted she had been *"too busy."* Work had picked up, her phone kept her scrolling late into the night, and her weekends were full. She never planned to drift from the Lord, but distraction slowly replaced devotion, and the door of intimacy with God began to close without her noticing.

That is the danger of a divided heart. *"Set your affection on things above, not on things on the earth"* (Colossians 3:2).

You cannot fix your heart on heaven if your mind is constantly pulled in a hundred directions. Martha learned this lesson in Luke 10 when she busied herself serving while Mary sat at Jesus' feet. Martha wasn't doing anything sinful. She was working hard for the Lord, but her busyness kept her from what mattered most. Jesus said, *"Martha, Martha, thou art careful and troubled about many things: But one thing is needful..."* (Luke 10:41–42). In that moment, distraction became the open door that kept her from deeper fellowship.

The Holy Spirit often speaks in these moments, not through thunder, but through the quiet conviction of the heart as He brings God's Word to mind (John 14:26; Psalm 119:11). If you ignore that nudge, distraction becomes distance, and distance gives the enemy room to whisper.

That's why the door of distraction must be closed quickly. Refocus and simplify. Identify what's keeping you from prayer, Scripture, and fellowship. Some things may need to be cut out entirely. Others must be put back in proper order. Time with God is not something to fit in when the schedule clears. It's the foundation that gives every other part of life meaning.

Spiritual Warfare: Building Your Battle Plan

When you close the door of distraction, you make space again to hear the Shepherd's voice. And when you hear His voice, the enemy's lies lose their volume.

Distraction feels harmless, but it opens the door to spiritual drift.

The Door of Secret Habits

Some of the hardest battles in the Christian life are the ones no one else can see. Secret habits keep believers in quiet bondage while everything looks fine on the outside.

I once counseled a woman who appeared strong in her faith. She came to church, carried her Bible, and knew all the right answers, even memorized several scriptures. But in private, she was feeding a habit she had never confessed. She thought she had control, but the habit was slowly controlling her thoughts, time, and heart. The more she hid it, the stronger it became, and the more it drained her joy.

Jesus said, "*...men loved darkness rather than light, because their deeds were evil*" (John 3:19). The devil thrives in darkness. He knows that as long as sin remains hidden, it can grow without resistance. David experienced this before Nathan confronted him: "*When I kept silence, my bones waxed old through my roaring all the day long*" (Psalm 32:3). Hidden sin wears you down from the inside out. It is like leaving the back door of your heart unlocked, an open invitation for the enemy to return again and again.

The Holy Spirit never ignores a secret sin. He faithfully convicts and calls the believer to repentance (John 16:8; Galatians 5:16). He convicts not to shame, but to free. When He exposes what is hidden, that light is mercy, not judgment. Bring the sin into the open with God first. Call it what it is, and then ask Him for courage to find accountability with a trusted believer. "*Confess your faults one to another, and pray one for another, that ye may be healed*" (James 5:16).

Accountability is not humiliation. It is protection. It is the spiritual safeguard that keeps you standing when temptation tries to return. When you close the door on secret habits, you stop giving the enemy a

Chapter 4: Preventing the Attack

place to work unseen in your soul. The light of God's truth floods in, cleansing what darkness tried to claim, and healing begins.

**Secret habits thrive in darkness.
Confession brings them into the light.**

The Door of Spiritual Neglect

One of the easiest doors to leave open is the door of neglect. It rarely swings wide in rebellion. It usually cracks open through routine and forgetfulness. Most believers do not rebel against God deliberately. They drift away slowly. Life grows busy, priorities shift, and the practices that once kept the heart close to the Lord begin to slip.

I remember a friend I had as a teenager. We grew up in church together, and after he got saved, he was on fire for God. He carried his Bible everywhere. He was in every youth service and every revival meeting, always eager to pray and share what the Lord was teaching him. As the years passed, his priorities began to change. Sports, friends, and weekend plans crowded out the things of God. One missed Sunday turned into several, and before long, the Bible that had once been open every day was gathering dust. When I saw him later and asked how he was doing spiritually, he said, *"I don't know what happened. I just don't feel close to God anymore."* The truth was simple. He had left the door of neglect wide open.

"Therefore we ought to give the more earnest heed to the things which we have heard, lest at any time we should let them slip" (Hebrews 2:1). That word slip paints the image of a boat drifting from shore, not pushed away, just quietly carried off by the current. That's how neglect opens the door to spiritual drift. You don't plan to wander, but you stop anchoring your heart daily, and before long the current carries you farther than you ever meant to go.

Peter did the same on the night of Jesus' arrest. He followed "afar off" (Luke 22:54). That distance made it easier for fear to take hold and for denial to follow. The same danger still exists today. The moment you begin following *"afar off,"* your strength fades and your guard lowers.

Spiritual Warfare: Building Your Battle Plan

The Holy Spirit will not allow neglect to sit comfortably. He stirs a holy restlessness, reminding you of what you once had and calling you to return. Respond quickly. Recommit to the basics: Sunday worship, daily prayer, time in the Word, and fellowship with believers. Strength to resist the enemy doesn't come from trying harder in the flesh. It comes from abiding in Christ, through the power of His indwelling Spirit (John 15:4–5; Philippians 4:13).

Closing the door of neglect is not about doing more religious things. It's about protecting your relationship with Christ so carefully that devotion stays fresh and distance never finds a foothold. When the heart stays close, the door stays shut.

Neglect opens the door slowly.
Daily devotion keeps it closed.

Shut the Door and Keep It Shut

When God shows you a door the enemy is using, don't wait until tomorrow to close it. The longer it stays open, the more ground the enemy gains. Think about it: if a wild animal wandered into your house, you wouldn't finish dinner before chasing it out. You would act immediately, slam the door, and lock it tight. In the same way, when sin or temptation slips in, delay only gives it time to destroy. That's exactly how you must respond in the spiritual realm.

You don't have to live in fear of the devil, but you must stop giving him a place to work. Every open door is an invitation, and he will always accept it. The Bible gives the order clearly: "*Submit yourselves therefore to God. Resist the devil, and he will flee from you*" (James 4:7). The enemy doesn't linger where he is resisted in the power of God's Spirit.

So how do you shut the door?

First, be honest with God. Call sin what it is and agree with Him about it, that's confession. Then, make the choice to walk away completely, that's repentance. Sometimes this means removing things from your life that keep drawing you back to weakness.

Next, fill the empty space with God's Word. The devil loves a vacuum, but he cannot stand where truth is planted. Finally, pray daily

Chapter 4: Preventing the Attack

for strength and stay connected with other believers. There is power in standing together.

The good news is that no door is beyond God's ability to close. No matter how long it has been open, He can cleanse, restore, and make you strong again. Victory is not about trying harder in your strength. It's about surrendering more fully to the power and lordship of Jesus Christ (2 Corinthians 2:14; Ephesians 6:10). When you close the door in His strength, keep it shut through obedience, and guard it with truth, the enemy loses his access, and peace takes its place.

Close the door quickly.
Guard it faithfully.

The Good News of Restoration

David knew what it was to fall and be restored. After his failure, he prayed, "*Create in me a clean heart, O God; and renew a right spirit within me*" (Psalm 51:10). God answered that prayer, and He still does.

When you bring every part of your heart to the Lord, He goes to work like a master craftsman, sweeping out the lies, removing the enemy's footholds, and sealing every crack with His grace. His restoration is not patchwork. It is complete renewal, strengthening you to walk in continual obedience and victory (2 Corinthians 12:9; Titus 2:11–12). And when His grace fills the room, the enemy finds no place left to stand.

That is the good news of restoration: you are not doomed to repeat old battles. The Spirit who convicts also cleanses, and the same power that closes the door keeps it shut, and keeps you standing.

God doesn't just close the doors.
He restores what the enemy damaged.

4

BUILD YOUR BATTLE PLAN

PREVENT THE ATTACK

Every open door in your life is an invitation for the enemy to set up camp. The good news? In Christ, you have real authority to slam them shut and keep them shut.

This section isn't optional. It's urgent. Pause right here. Get alone with the Lord. Ask Him to shine His light into every corner, every hidden place. Ask Him to expose any area where access has been left open, whether through sin, compromise, neglect, or avoidance. Moving forward without closing doors leaves you fighting from a weakened position.

> *"Neither give place to the devil."*
> ***Ephesians 4:27***

Purpose of This Battle Plan

This plan is designed to help you:
- Identify the small openings the enemy uses to gain access.
- Close those doors quickly through obedience and repentance.
- Guard vulnerable areas before they become strongholds.
- Establish protective habits that limit future attacks.

Step 1: Identify the Open Door

You've already recognized the attack and started responding God's way. But the enemy didn't just wander in. He found a door that was cracked open, and he's been working through it. This step focuses on how the enemy gained access.

Review the chapter and identify any door that may be open.

1. Check all that apply:
   - ☐ Unconfessed sin
   - ☐ Bitterness or unforgiveness
   - ☐ Distraction from spiritual priorities
   - ☐ Secret habits or hidden sin
   - ☐ Spiritual neglect (prayer, Scripture, church)
   - ☐ Other: _____

2. What evidence tells you this door is open?
   (Behavior, pressure point, repeated struggle, loss of peace, conviction)

Step 2: Agree With God About It

Spotting the open door is only half the battle. The door remains open until you agree with God about what it is. Awareness alone does not shut it. Agreement does.

God does not require emotion, explanation, or self-analysis. He requires honesty. Until you call the issue what He calls it, the door stays cracked, and the enemy retains access.

How to do it?

In writing, name the issue truthfully before God.

- *Don't soften the language.*
- *Don't justify it or explain why it exists.*
- *Don't shift blame to circumstances, other people, or pressure.*

Call it exactly what God calls it. Agreement means aligning your judgment with His, without defense or delay.

Now It's Your Turn:

Write the sentence below and complete it honestly. Say it aloud. Let your own voice agree with God. This is the moment where excuse ends and obedience begins.

"Lord, I agree with You about _____."

Continue writing below. Do not rush. Keep going until everything the Spirit brings to the surface has been named clearly and without restraint.

Step 3: Confess and Turn from It

Identifying the open door and agreeing with God about it are necessary steps, but the door does not fully close until confession and repentance take place. Agreement aligns your judgment with God's. Confession and repentance change your direction.

How to do it?

Write a short, direct prayer of confession.

Include these three things:
- Name exactly what you are confessing.
- State your decision to turn from it.
- Express dependence on God's grace, not your own strength.

Example (to guide you, not to copy): *"Lord, I confess my bitterness toward [name] as sin. I choose right now to forgive and release them. I can't do this in my own strength. I'm depending completely on Your grace to change my heart and help me walk in obedience. In Jesus' name, amen."*

Now It's Your Turn:

Write your prayer below. Be specific. Then pray it aloud to God.

Step 4: Remove What Keeps the Door Open

Some doors do not stay open by accident. They are being held open by something concrete: a habit, an access point, a pattern, or a repeated choice. As long as that remains in place, the enemy retains access.

If you identify the door but leave the prop in place, the door will reopen. Removal is what allows it to close completely.

How to do it?

Identify what must be removed, restricted, or cut off immediately. Write only what applies to you. Be specific. This is not a brainstorming exercise. It is a decision-making moment.

1. Something to delete or discard.
   (apps, sites, files, books, items, subscriptions):

2. A boundary that must be set.
   (with people, places, times, media):

3. A habit that must be interrupted.
   (daily routines, thought patterns, default responses):

4. A relationship dynamic that must change.
   (conversations, access, enabling patterns):

5. A pattern that must be confronted.
   (procrastination, avoidance, cycles, excuses):

You are not trying to earn God's favor. You are guarding what He has already given you. Removing access is how you deny the enemy a foothold and preserve clarity, peace, and spiritual authority.

Step 5: Fill the Space with Truth and Obedience

Closing the door and removing what held it open is real progress. This step is about replacement. Whatever was removed must be intentionally replaced with something God-directed, life-giving, and sustainable. If nothing takes its place, the old nature will attempt to return.

How to do it?

Answer the following questions clearly and specifically. Write them as commitments, not ideas. These answers become part of your standing Battle Plan.

1. What spiritual practice will replace what was removed?
   Examples may include:
   - *Daily time in the Word at a set time.*
   - *Scripture memory connected to this area.*
   - *Targeted prayer over this issue.*
   - *Regular accountability with a trusted believer.*

2. Write your commitment:

3. What Scripture will guard this area?
   Choose one verse or short passage that directly speaks truth into this space. Write it out fully. This is the truth you will return to whenever the attack tries to reopen the door.

4. Write the Scripture here:

PART THREE

THE BATTLEFIELD

*The war is real,
but you are not unarmed.*

5

THE BATTLEGROUND

*Before the enemy conquers your life,
he first captures your thoughts.*

You've learned how to respond when the enemy strikes. But the battle you face isn't always visible. It's fought inside your mind. No one else hears the thoughts that wear you down or the doubts that whisper when the room grows quiet. Yet that unseen conflict shapes everything about how you live. The enemy, Satan, knows that if he can control your thoughts, he can weaken your faith. But God has given you power through His Spirit to fight back, and though the battle is in your mind, the victory comes only from Him. *"For the weapons of our warfare are not carnal, but mighty through God to the pulling down of strong holds; Casting down imaginations, and every high thing that exalteth itself against the knowledge of God, and bringing into captivity every thought to the obedience of Christ"* (2 Corinthians 10:4–5). *"...Greater is he that is in you, than he that is in the world"* (1 John 4:4)

These verses remind us that the battle is not fought with human weapons, but with divine power that pulls down every stronghold of thought. Victory begins where transformation begins, within. That's

Spiritual Warfare: Building Your Battle Plan

why Scripture says, *"...Be not conformed to this world: but be ye transformed by the renewing of your mind"* (Romans 12:2).

I've seen believers just like you who look strong on the outside. Bill came to church every Sunday, served faithfully, smiled when spoken to, bowed his head in prayer. But inside, his thoughts had turned against him. Every night when the lights went out, another voice whispered, *"You're a failure. You'll never be what you were. God's finished with you."*

The whispers felt real. He tried to ignore them, quoting a few verses and calling it stress, but the more he resisted, the louder they grew. His joy began to fade, his prayer life grew quiet, and he no longer had a desire to read his Bible.

One Sunday, his pew stayed empty. Bill wasn't rebellious, just weary, weary of fighting an invisible enemy that lived inside his thoughts. Many believers know that feeling. On the outside, they keep moving, but inside, they're at war. The fiercest battles are often fought in our minds, where no one else can hear.

Spiritual warfare doesn't always sound like thunder. It often comes quietly, disguised as ordinary thoughts.

The fiercest battles are fought in your mind, where no one else can hear.

The War in the Mind

Most of the battles you face will never be seen by others. They are fought in silence in the hidden conversations of the heart and mind. Every temptation begins as a thought, and every doubt begins as a whisper. The enemy doesn't need to storm your life when he can quietly slip into your thinking.

That is why the Bible calls you to let God reshape your thinking: *"And be renewed in the spirit of your mind"* (Ephesians 4:23). Victory always begins where God's power renews what the enemy attacked, in the mind.

From the very beginning, Satan's weapon was not a sword but a sentence, words that twisted what God said: *"Yea, hath God said...?"* (Genesis 3:1). He didn't deny God's Word. He distorted it. He didn't

Chapter 5: The Battleground

challenge God's power. He questioned God's heart. With one question, he planted doubt in Eve's mind, and that doubt became disobedience.

That is still how he works today. He knows that if he can shape your thoughts, he can shape your life. If he can plant a lie, he can weaken your faith. But God has not left you defenseless. *"For God hath not given us the spirit of fear; but of power, and of love, and of a sound mind"* (2 Timothy 1:7).

A sound mind is anchored in truth, steady, disciplined, and unmoved by fear. When your mind is anchored, your life follows. The enemy cannot claim your heart, but he can persuade your thoughts. He cannot control your future, but he can cloud your focus. He cannot rule your life, but he can rattle your confidence.

This is why the battle matters so much. Every victory begins with truth believed, and every defeat begins when truth is doubted. The war in the mind determines the strength of your walk with God. That's why the Bible calls you to reject every thought that opposes the knowledge of God and to fill the mind with what is true: *"Finally, brethren, whatsoever things are true, whatsoever things are honest, whatsoever things are just, whatsoever things are pure, whatsoever things are lovely, whatsoever things are of good report; if there be any virtue, and if there be any praise, think on these things"* (Philippians 4:8).

**The war in your mind determines
the strength of your walk.**

Recognizing the Real Battlefield

When life begins to unravel, most people look outward for someone to blame. They point to people, circumstances, or life's pressures. But the believer who understands spiritual warfare looks inward first. *"For the weapons of our warfare are not carnal, but mighty through God to the pulling down of strong holds; Casting down imaginations, and every high thing that exalteth itself against the knowledge of God, and bringing into captivity every thought to the obedience of Christ"* (2 Corinthians 10:4–5).

These strongholds are not physical buildings or habits you can see.

Spiritual Warfare: Building Your Battle Plan

They are patterns of thinking that have become fortified against the knowledge of God. They are lies from the enemy that have been believed long enough to feel like truth, holding you captive and resisting God's Word. It's not every passing doubt or negative thought. It's when those lies dig in deep, build walls, and start governing how you see God, yourself, and your life.

Strongholds form quietly. They begin as thoughts you accept without challenging. Over time, they harden into assumptions. And eventually, they shape your behavior, keeping sin or bondage in place. They convince you that change is impossible, that God's promises don't apply to you, or that you'll never break free. But through Christ, every stronghold can be torn down.

Think of a man who grew up hearing he'd never amount to anything. Words from family, teachers, failures piled up. Even after he got saved, that lie stayed rooted. He'd read *"I can do all things through Christ which strengtheneth me"* (Philippians 4:13), but in his mind, a voice always answered, *"Not you. You're the exception."* He served in church, but never stepped into more. He prayed, but never expected big answers. That lie wasn't loud. It was quiet, constant, and crippling. It was a stronghold, a fortress of unbelief built brick by brick from old words he never replaced with truth.

That's how strongholds work. They're not the sin itself. They're the lies protecting the sin, making it feel unbreakable. The addiction, the anger, the fear, they stay because the underlying lie feels like truth.

When the walls of Jericho fell, it wasn't the shout that held the power, but the obedience that trusted God's command. In the same way, obedience to truth always topples lies believed. The Word of God breaks the walls of deception and restores the mind to truth. *"So then faith cometh by hearing, and hearing by the word of God"* (Romans 10:17).

Before you can fight effectively, you must recognize where the battle is truly taking place. The greatest danger isn't what is happening around you, but what is happening within you. Pulling weeds from a garden may make it look clean for a moment, just as pushing away wrong thoughts can seem like victory, but unless the roots are removed, they return stronger. The same is true of thoughts that are never replaced by truth.

Chapter 5: The Battleground

The war for your mind cannot be won by determination or discipline alone. It is won by the truth of Christ and His Word that disarms every lie and strengthens you. *"Jesus saith unto him, I am the way, the truth, and the life: no man cometh unto the Father, but by me"* (John 14:6). *"Sanctify them through thy truth: thy word is truth"* (John 17:17). *"And take the helmet of salvation, and the sword of the Spirit, which is the word of God"* (Ephesians 6:17).

Strongholds are lies that feel like truth.
Truth is the only thing that tears them down.

The First Lie Ever Told

Every believer must understand where this war truly begins. The fiercest battles are not fought on the outside. They are fought within your mind. The enemy knows that if he can influence your thinking, he can influence your actions. That is why the mind remains his favorite battleground.

When Jesus was tempted in the wilderness, Satan attacked through words, not weapons of war. Each lie was met with Scripture, and every time, truth drove the deceiver away. His first weapon was not a spear. It was a subtle question of doubt.

"*Yea, hath God said...?*" (Genesis 3:1)

With one question, Satan planted doubt in Eve's mind. He didn't need to shout. He only needed to cause her to wonder whether God's Word could be trusted. That single moment of hesitation opened the door to deception. Many believers lose spiritual ground the same way, not through rebellion, but through hesitation. The moment you pause to question what you already know to be true, the battle begins to turn (Genesis 3:1–6; 2 Corinthians 11:3).

He did not deny what God said. He distorted it. He twisted truth until obedience felt like restriction and rebellion looked like freedom. *"When he speaketh a lie, he speaketh of his own: for he is a liar, and the father of it"* (John 8:44). The same voice that deceived Eve still whispers today. He still suggests that God is holding something back,

Spiritual Warfare: Building Your Battle Plan

that God's way is too narrow, His commands too burdensome, and His blessings too slow.

But Scripture answers clearly: *"Every good gift and every perfect gift is from above, and cometh down from the Father of lights, with whom is no variableness, neither shadow of turning"* (James 1:17). The Giver of every good thing withholds nothing that is best. If the devil can make you question God's goodness, obedience will soon crumble.

That is who the devil is, deception personified. He does not simply tell lies. He embodies them, and every part of his nature is false. Every thought he plants carries spiritual death at its root. The lie in the Garden is the same lie he tells today: You can have what you desire without obeying God's will. It sounded promising, but it poisoned everything it touched, and it still does (Genesis 3:5–6; 1 John 2:16).

The first battle ever fought was for a single thought. That battle still rages today.

What the Devil Can and Cannot Do

Fear grows when you don't understand the enemy's limits. When you forget what he can and cannot do, you give him more credit than he deserves. The devil is real. He is active. He is powerful. But he is not supreme. Understanding his limits frees you from unnecessary fear and prepares your heart for victory.

The Devil Is Not All-Knowing

Only God knows everything: *"For there is not a word in my tongue, but, lo, O LORD, thou knowest it altogether"* (Psalm 139:4). The enemy cannot read your thoughts or know your future. He learns by watching, by studying patterns, by listening to what you say. He's not omniscient. He's a creature, limited and fallen.

I've counseled believers who lived terrified, thinking Satan knew every secret in their heart. They'd say, *"Pastor, he knows what I'm thinking—he's always one step ahead."* But that's not true. He guesses, he suggests, he accuses based on what he sees. But he doesn't

Chapter 5: The Battleground

know your heart like God does. Bring those thoughts to the Lord in prayer, and the enemy loses his guesswork advantage.

The Devil Cannot Possess A Child Of God

Once you belong to Christ, you are sealed and secured. *"...Greater is he that is in you, than he that is in the world"* (1 John 4:4). *"For ye are bought with a price"* (1 Corinthians 6:20). The Holy Spirit doesn't share space. He takes full ownership. Light and darkness cannot live in the same temple.

In Scripture, Jesus cast demons out of unbelievers, never out of His own disciples. The indwelling Spirit and a demonic spirit cannot inhabit the same life. The devil may oppress from the outside, harass, accuse, tempt, but he cannot possess from within. His weapons are lies and pressure, not ownership. Possession is impossible for a believer. Oppression is defeated by standing in faith. *"Above all, taking the shield of faith, wherewith ye shall be able to quench all the fiery darts of the wicked"* (Ephesians 6:16).

Your protection isn't in your own strength. It's in the indwelling Spirit of God.

The Devil Is Not All-Powerful

He is mighty, but he is not Almighty. Remember Job: *"...Behold, all that he hath is in thy power; only upon himself put not forth thine hand"* (Job 1:12). Even in his worst attacks, Satan operates under God's sovereign limit.

Satan cannot act without permission. He may roar like a lion, but his chain is short. He can tempt, but he cannot force. He can accuse, but he cannot condemn. *"Who shall lay any thing to the charge of God's elect? It is God that justifieth"* (Romans 8:33). He can wound, but he cannot win. *"...Resist the devil, and he will flee from you"* (James 4:7).

Submission to God breaks fear's hold. Faith doesn't ignore the devil. It refuses to tremble before him.

Spiritual Warfare: Building Your Battle Plan

The Devil Cannot Stop the Work of God

"*...My counsel shall stand, and I will do all my pleasure*" (Isaiah 46:10). Every time Satan thinks he's won, God turns it for good. He used Judas's betrayal to bring redemption. He used persecution to scatter the church, and that scattering spread the gospel.

Acts 8:4 says when believers fled Jerusalem, "*...they that were scattered abroad went every where preaching the word.*" The enemy scattered them. God multiplied them.

The enemy cannot stop what God has ordained. He may delay, distract, deceive, but he cannot destroy God's plan. What God starts, He finishes, every time.

> **The devil is loud, but he is limited.**
> **He is cunning, but he is constrained.**

Living Confident in His Limits

Knowing the enemy's limits brings confidence, not carelessness. He cannot read your thoughts, possess your soul, or touch your salvation. He cannot overrule your Savior, and he cannot stop the plan of God.

He is loud, but limited. Cunning, but constrained. Fallen, but finished. "*And the devil that deceived them was cast into the lake of fire*" (Revelation 20:10). The devil's reach stops where God's permission ends, just like in Job's trial (Job 1:12). When you know that truth, it removes fear and replaces it with faith. Once you understand his limits, you can face his attacks without intimidation or doubt.

I've seen believers live paralyzed because they thought the devil was bigger than he is. But when they grasped these truths, something shifted. Peace returned. Boldness grew. They stopped trembling and started standing.

You don't have to fear an enemy who's already defeated. You just have to trust the God who defeated him.

> **Fear grows in what you don't understand.**
> **Truth sets you free.**

Chapter 5: The Battleground

The Fiery Darts of the Enemy

Every believer faces the same pattern of attack. The devil knows he cannot control your mind, but he can press against it with temptation and lies. His strategy is simple: plant lies that stir emotion and weaken faith (1 Corinthians 10:13; 2 Corinthians 11:3).

A fiery dart does not come from within you. It is launched from without. These darts arrive as thoughts, whispers, and *"what-ifs"*, small, burning suggestions meant to pierce peace and consume confidence. They come suddenly, like sparks from an unseen hand, but faith lifted quickly like a shield is enough to keep them from catching fire.

"Above all, taking the shield of faith, wherewith ye shall be able to quench all the fiery darts of the wicked" (Ephesians 6:16).

Like flaming arrows striking a shield, the lies can be stopped, but only by faith that trusts what God has said over what feelings suggest. Satan's arsenal is not vast, but it is effective. Most of his darts fall into four familiar categories: doubt, accusation, fear, and discouragement.

The Dart of Doubt

The first dart ever fired was doubt. *"Yea, hath God said...?"* (Genesis 3:1). He still whispers the same words today: *"Maybe God didn't mean that promise for you."* Doubt creates hesitation. It keeps you caught halfway between faith and fear.

Peter stepped out of the boat in faith, but when doubt entered, he began to sink. Yet the same Lord who rebuked the wind also reached out His hand and lifted him again. Doubt can drown you quickly, but faith can rescue you instantly.

"If the Son therefore shall make you free, ye shall be free indeed" (John 8:36).

**When faith declares what God has written,
the spark of doubt dies before it can spread.**

Spiritual Warfare: Building Your Battle Plan

The Dart of Accusation

If doubt questions God, accusation questions you. The enemy points to your past and whispers, *"You've failed too much to be used again."*

Amber learned that truth one evening in Bible study. She had been quiet all night until she finally said, *"I know God forgave me, but I can't seem to forgive myself."* Her friend opened her Bible and read, *"It is of the LORD's mercies that we are not consumed, because his compassions fail not. They are new every morning: great is thy faithfulness"* (Lamentations 3:22–23).

Those words sank deep. The next morning, Amber taped that verse to her mirror. Every time the whisper returned, she answered it with Scripture. Zechariah saw Joshua the high priest standing before the angel of the Lord, and Satan stood to accuse him. But the Lord said, *"...the LORD rebuke thee, O Satan"* (Zechariah 3:2).

Mercy spoke louder than accusation then, and it still does now. The same accusation that once ruled her mind lost its power under truth.

**An accusation cannot stand
where mercy is believed.**

The Dart of Fear

Fear is one of the enemy's loudest lies. He paints worst-case pictures that feel real long before they happen: *"What if the report is bad? What if God doesn't come through this time?"* Fear is faith in reverse. It believes the lie instead of the Lord.

When the storm rose on the Sea of Galilee, the disciples cried out in fear. Then Jesus said, *"It is I; be not afraid."* The wind still howled, but their hearts quieted at His word.

"For God hath not given us the spirit of fear; but of power, and of love, and of a sound mind" (2 Timothy 1:7). When faith speaks that verse out loud, fear's fire fades. God never sends a spirit of fear, and He never abandons His children to it.

Chapter 5: The Battleground

The Dart of Discouragement

When Satan cannot make you sin, he tries to make you stop. Discouragement drains strength one thought at a time: *"You've prayed enough. You've tried enough. You'll never see change."*

Elijah sat under the juniper tree, weary and ready to quit. But God met him there with food, rest, and a fresh word. What despair had taken, divine strength restored.

"Being confident of this very thing, that he which hath begun a good work in you will perform it until the day of Jesus Christ." (Philippians 1:6) Discouragement dies when you remember that God finishes what He starts. You are not running alone, and you are not running in vain.

Discouragement dies when you remember God finishes what He starts.

How to Defend the Mind

Once you recognize the devil's attacks, defending yourself begins with what fills it. The enemy aims for your thoughts, but God has already given you everything you need to stand firm. Victory never comes by accident. It comes by spiritual preparation. That preparation begins in the mind.

These four defenses turn knowledge into victory and truth into strength.

1. Fill Your Mind with God's Word

   "...It is written, Man shall not live by bread alone, but by every word that proceedeth out of the mouth of God." (Matthew 4:4) When Jesus faced temptation, He didn't argue with the devil. He answered him. Each time Satan spoke, Jesus replied, *"It is written."* No opinions, no excuses, just the Word, precise and powerful. That is still your greatest defense.

Spiritual Warfare: Building Your Battle Plan

A mind full of God's Word leaves little room for lies. When the world fills your thoughts with fear, speak the promises of God aloud. When temptation whispers, respond with what is written. The more you know His Word, the faster you silence the enemy.

The Word is not a last resort. It is your first line of defense. Make it personal. Write down verses that speak directly to your struggle. Keep them where you can see them: on your phone, your dashboard, your mirror. The more the Word fills your mind, the less room there is for the enemy's lies.

2. *Guard What You Allow In*

"Keep thy heart with all diligence; for out of it are the issues of life." (Proverbs 4:23) A guarded mind is a peaceful mind. You cannot fill your thoughts with darkness and expect to walk in light. A believer who feeds constantly on the noise of the world will struggle to hear the still, small voice of God.

Guard what you watch, what you listen to, and what you dwell on. Everything you allow in will either strengthen your faith or weaken it. Be the gatekeeper of your thoughts. Walking away from a conversation that dishonors Christ or turning off a show that stirs temptation is already raising the shield of faith. Guarding the mind is not silence. It is choosing carefully what you let in.

You cannot leave your door open to the world and still expect peace to stay inside. A guarded mind is not empty. It is occupied by truth.

3. *Pray for a Renewed Mind*

"And the peace of God, which passeth all understanding, shall keep your hearts and minds through Christ Jesus." (Philippians 4:7) Renewal is not self-improvement. It is surrender. It begins when you yield your thoughts in prayer. Worry cannot live where prayer is active. Fear cannot rule where faith is spoken.

Chapter 5: The Battleground

Ask the Lord to cleanse your thoughts daily and to guard your focus. David prayed, *"Search me, O God, and know my heart: try me, and know my thoughts"* (Psalm 139:23). That is where a renewed mind begins, with honesty before God.

A renewed mind does not come by accident. It comes by surrender to the Holy Spirit. Scripture reminds us, *"Set your affection on things above, not on things on the earth"* (Colossians 3:2). When prayer replaces panic, peace follows.

4. *Surround Yourself with God's People*

"And let us consider one another to provoke unto love and to good works." (Hebrews 10:24) You were never meant to fight alone. Isolation leaves the mind unguarded. Fellowship strengthens faith and reminds you of the truth when you forget it.

When Moses' arms grew weary on the hill, Aaron and Hur held them up until the battle was won (Exodus 17:11–12). God still strengthens His people through the hands of others. Stay close to believers who pray for you, who speak truth when you waver, who will not let you fall without a fight.

Encouragement from God's people is often the shield God uses to block the next dart of doubt or fear. When you walk in fellowship, you walk in strength.

You're not meant to fight alone.
God gave you the church for a reason.

Winning the War in Your Mind

The battle for your mind is real, but so is the victory God promises. You are not fighting alone, and you are not fighting for victory. You are fighting from it. *"But thanks be to God, which giveth us the victory through our Lord Jesus Christ"* (1 Corinthians 15:57). The blood of Christ has already secured the outcome. Now you live in the reality of that victory.

Spiritual Warfare: Building Your Battle Plan

Like David standing before Goliath, confidence does not come from size or skill. It comes from knowing the Lord has already delivered the victory. The enemy may roar, but his defeat is certain. Christ has already conquered every lie with truth, every accusation with mercy, and every fear with faith (Hebrews 2:14; Colossians 2:15).

The believer's story is not one of defeat but of endurance. When you respond in faith, the battle may still rage, but the victory, already secured by Christ's finished work, is simply claimed by faith.

Bill learned this truth when he stopped believing the guilt and started believing in God's grace. Amber discovered it when she replaced shame with mercy. Each of them found that victory was not achieved by effort. It was accepted by faith.

When Israel stood before the Red Sea, deliverance did not come by pushing forward, but by trusting God to part what no strength could move. *"Nay, in all these things we are more than conquerors through him that loved us"* (Romans 8:37).

The believer who renews his mind daily does more than survive temptation. He overcomes it. He walks in freedom, not fear. He thinks with clarity, not confusion. Every thought that once enslaved him now becomes a testimony of God's power to transform.

You are not fighting for victory.
You are fighting from victory.

Taking Every Thought Captive

"Finally, brethren, whatsoever things are true... think on these things." (Philippians 4:8) This is how you take thoughts captive: replace every lie with what is true, honest, just, pure, lovely, and of good report. Victory in the mind begins when truth becomes the filter for every thought. Before reacting to a hurtful word or fearful idea, remember what Scripture says, choosing obedience over emotion. That single moment of surrender changes the outcome.

You do not silence thoughts by effort. You surrender them by obedience. You do not win by emptying your mind, but by filling it with truth. The believer who filters every thought through the Word of God will no longer be a slave to lies.

Chapter 5: The Battleground

When doubt whispers, truth answers. When fear speaks, faith replies. When guilt returns, grace stands its ground. Victory in the mind is not sinless perfection. It is daily submission to Christ through the truth of His Word. *"Sanctify them through thy truth: thy word is truth"* (John 17:17). *"Submit yourselves therefore to God. Resist the devil, and he will flee from you"* (James 4:7).

The Peace That Stays

The peace Paul described still holds true, the same peace of God that passes all understanding now guards your heart like a soldier at his post (Philippians 4:7). It's not peace that visits and leaves. It's peace that stays, surrounding every thought with the presence of Christ Himself.

Peace is not the absence of battle. It is the presence of Christ in the middle of it. That peace does not prevent the enemy's approach. It prevents his entry. When your thoughts are anchored in truth, peace stands guard like a soldier at the gate.

Paul and Silas sang hymns in the prison at midnight. The chains were still on, but peace had already entered the cell. That same peace can dwell in every believer who keeps his mind fixed on the Lord. The storm may rage, but the heart remains still because peace has taken its post.

Peace is the presence of Christ in the middle of the battle.

From Captive to Conqueror

The believer whose mind is stayed on God becomes unshakable because his peace no longer depends on circumstance. It rests on Christ alone.

Every attack that once brought fear now builds faith. Every lie that once weakened you now reminds you of victory. Every thought that once distracted you now draws you closer to Christ.

The battlefield of your mind can become a sanctuary of peace when Christ and His truth reign there. The war ends where truth is believed and peace begins. The victory is not distant. It is daily. And it is already yours in Christ.

"*The truth shall make you free... If the Son therefore shall make you free, ye shall be free indeed*" (John 8:32–36). "*And let the peace of God rule in your hearts*" (Colossians 3:15).

The battlefield of your mind becomes a sanctuary when Christ reigns there.

5

BUILD YOUR BATTLE PLAN

THE BATTLEGROUND

You can map out every scheme of the enemy, understand exactly how he twists thoughts, plants doubt, and stirs up lies, but if that knowledge stays in your head and never moves to your hands and feet, nothing changes. Truth that lives only in theory leaves plenty of room for lies to come right back in and set up camp again.

The war in your mind isn't going to be won by awareness alone. It's won by deliberate, day-after-day obedience by taking everything you've learned and using it to stand firm where the enemy has been hitting you hardest.

What comes next isn't optional exercises or helpful ideas. It's your move. This is how truth becomes a weapon and ground is held, not lost. No more theorizing. It's time to fight the right way.

Purpose of this Battle Plan

The purpose of this battle plan is to help you confront the war in your mind with clarity, authority, and obedience to God's Word.

This plan is designed to train you to:

- Identify hostile thoughts before they take root.
- Reject lies without negotiation.
- Replace deception with Scripture-based truth.
- Maintain mental ground through disciplined, daily practice.

Step 1: Identify The Thought Under Attack

You can't fight what you refuse to name. The enemy's biggest advantage is staying anonymous. Allowing hostile thoughts to move through your mind as if they are simply *your thoughts, normal, natural, or harmless.*

This step is about dragging those thoughts into the light and calling them what they are: hostile fire aimed at your faith, your peace, and your walk with God.

How to do it?

Right now, write down the recurring thought (or thoughts) that have been weakening your faith, stealing your joy, or pulling you away from trust in God. Be specific.

Examples:
"God isn't going to come through for me this time."
"I'm too broken for God to ever really use me."
"Nobody truly cares, and I'll always end up alone."

1. Write the exact thought here:

2. Does this thought agree with what God has said in His Word, or does it directly oppose it?

If your thought contradicts who God is, what He has promised, or who you are in Christ, then it is not from Him. Period.

No matter how loud it feels.
No matter how familiar it sounds.
No matter how much *"evidence"* your circumstances seem to give it.

This step exposes the real battlefield. Once the thought is named and seen for what it is, enemy fire, you are no longer fighting in the dark. You are positioned to stand. Do this now. Name it clearly. The fight starts here.

Step 2: Reject The Lie Without Debate

Lies do not gain power because they are intelligent. They gain power because they are entertained, because they are allowed to linger, explain themselves, or argue their case in your mind. The moment you begin debating a lie, you have already given it ground.

Truth works differently. Truth gains power the moment it is declared, out loud, without hesitation.

You do not reason with deceptive thoughts.
You do not negotiate with them.
You confront them and cast them down.

How to do it?

Take the exact hostile thought you named in Step 1.
Right now, speak this out loud (hear your own voice say it):

"This thought does not come from God, and I reject it in Jesus' name."

Then write that same sentence here. You may personalize it slightly if needed, but keep it short, direct, and decisive:

Then, if the lie tries to talk back, if it pushes harder, resurfaces, or throws *"evidence"* at you, repeat it again!

Step 3: Replace The Lie with Scripture

An empty mind isn't a defended mind. Casting out a lie is only half the battle. If you leave the space empty, the enemy will circle back and press again. Every lie must be replaced with truth, not your truth, not positive thinking, not vague encouragement, but with God's truth.

How to do it?

Return to the hostile thought you identified and rejected in **Steps 1** and **2**. Now find one verse of Scripture that directly contradicts it. Head-on, no compromise. Do not choose a general phrase that sounds comforting. Choose a clear promise, command, or declaration from God that destroys the lie.

Write the verse out in full here (reference included):

Then, directly beneath it, write this one sentence (you may personalize it slightly, but keep the meaning intact): *"This is what God says, and I submit my thoughts to it."*

Now read that verse out loud slowly and deliberately. Let your ears hear your voice declare what God has said. If the lie tries to surge back with fear, accusation, or *"evidence,"* read the verse again. Louder if you must.

"So then faith cometh by hearing, and hearing by the word of God" (Romans 10:17).

When you speak God's truth out loud, you begin rebuilding your mind on ground the enemy cannot hold. The lie loses its place when truth moves in and takes over.

6

THE WEAPONS

*The battle is fought with faith,
but won with the Word.*

You've learned how to recognize the attack and how to respond when it comes. But no soldier steps onto the battlefield unarmed. God never sends His children into war without weapons. He's equipped you with divine tools strong enough to pull down strongholds, silence the enemy's lies, and set you free. The problem isn't that you lack weapons. It's that many believers never learn how to use them.

Some live in defense mode, reacting instead of advancing in faith. Others know the Word but stop short of applying it. Many pray only when trouble comes, rather than from a steady walk with God.

That's why this chapter is so important. It's time to pick up what God has already placed in your hands.

**You're not a helpless target.
You're a trained soldier.**

Spiritual Warfare: Building Your Battle Plan

This isn't about human strength or religious emotion. It's about divine empowerment. Truth, prayer, praise, and obedience work together under Christ's authority, forming a steady rhythm of victory in your daily life.

Before any weapon is lifted, strength must come from the right source. Paul reminded the Ephesians, *"...be strong in the Lord, and in the power of his might. Put on the whole armour of God, that ye may be able to stand against the wiles of the devil"* (Ephesians 6:10–11).

Notice that he did not say, *"Be strong in yourself,"* but *"be strong in the Lord."* Victory begins not in determination, but in dependence on the Lord.

Your strength is not in who you are, but in whose you are, belonging to Christ. You do not fight for God. You fight in His strength and under His authority. When a believer fights from that position, confidence replaces fear, and peace becomes power.

Every weapon God provides serves a purpose. The Word of God cuts through deception. Prayer calls heaven's power to earth. Praise confuses the enemy and strengthens your heart. The blood of Christ removes every accusation. Confession closes open doors. Obedience leads to victory.

These weapons work because their power is divine, not human. They break chains, silence lies, and turn the battlefield of your heart from fear into faith.

> **The same God who fought for Joshua, Gideon, and Paul now fights for you.**

So before we begin, remember this: you are not unarmed, you are not untrained, and you are not abandoned. The same God who fought for Joshua, Gideon, and Paul now fights for you. All He asks is that you take up what He has already placed in your hands and use it.

Now that you know where the fight happens, it is time to take up your first weapon.

The Word of God: The Sword of the Spirit

Every soldier needs a weapon that can strike back, and for you, that

Chapter 6: The Weapons

weapon is not made of steel or earthly fire, but of truth itself. Paul described it when he said, "*...and the sword of the Spirit, which is the word of God*" (Ephesians 6:17).

The Word of God is your primary offensive weapon. It doesn't merely defend. It divides, exposes, and conquers. When every other piece of armor guards, this one strikes. Scripture reminds you that "*...the word of God is quick, and powerful, and sharper than any twoedged sword*" (Hebrews 4:12).

The Bible holds no power when it sits on a shelf and gathers dust. It was never meant to be carried as decoration. It was meant to cut through deception and expose the lies of the enemy. Like a soldier's blade, it must be sharpened and skillfully handled through daily use, in study, memorization, and obedience. A sword kept in its sheath cannot protect or prevail. But in your hand, trained and ready, it becomes unstoppable.

From the beginning, the devil's greatest weapon has been the lie. His deception thrives wherever truth is neglected or left unspoken. That is why the Word must come first among your weapons, because lies always strike first among his. When you know the Word, you know truth. When you speak the Word in faith, the Spirit empowers that truth against the enemy.

I have experienced this firsthand. There was a season when discouragement pressed hard, and lies about my calling kept whispering at night. I'd wake up heavy, questioning everything. But I started a simple habit: every morning, before anything else, I'd read a chapter out loud and write down one verse that spoke to me. Over weeks, those verses piled up. When the lies hit, I'd pull out my notebook and read them aloud. The whispers didn't stop overnight, but they lost their grip. Peace returned. Strength returned. That's the power of the Word. It doesn't just inform your mind. It transforms your heart.

When the enemy whispers, *"You're defeated,"* God's Word declares, "*Nay, in all these things we are more than conquerors through him that loved us*" (Romans 8:37). When guilt tries to take hold, the Word answers, "*There is therefore now no condemnation to them which are in Christ Jesus*" (Romans 8:1). Truth not only defends your mind. It renews it.

Spiritual Warfare: Building Your Battle Plan

When Satan tempted Jesus in the wilderness, He didn't debate or reason with the enemy. He simply spoke truth. He said, *"It is written..."* (Matthew 4:4, 7, 10), silencing Satan by declaring Scripture with authority.

That same authority rests in your hands. When you speak God's Word in faith, you resist the enemy, and he must flee according to God's promise (James 4:7). The enemy doesn't flee because of your tone or volume, but because of the authority behind the Word you speak.

But you must know His Word to wield its power. An unused sword dulls quickly. If you want to fight effectively, the Word must live in your heart, mind, and mouth. Memorize it. Meditate on it. Declare it when the enemy attacks. You don't have to shout for Scripture to show its power. Volume doesn't give it authority. Faith does. Its power comes from God, not from us.

The only way to sharpen your sword is through daily reading, memorizing, and meditating on Scripture. The goal is not to check off a list, but to prepare for battle. A whispered Scripture carries more authority than your loudest opinion, because its power lies not in your tone, but in God's truth.

When temptation strikes, speak the Word. When fear rises, quote the Word aloud. When doubt tries to take root, declare what God has already said. Every time you speak truth, your spirit strengthens and the enemy retreats. *"So shall my word be that goeth forth out of my mouth: it shall not return unto me void, but it shall accomplish that which I please, and it shall prosper in the thing whereto I sent it"* (Isaiah 55:11).

Every believer carries the same sword, but not every believer practices with it, by reading, meditating, and applying it. The more you handle the Word, the more natural it becomes in the battle. The Holy Spirit will bring to remembrance what you have hidden in your heart (John 14:26).

You are not powerless, for you hold the most effective weapon in all creation, the Word that spoke the universe into existence.

The sword is in your hands. The only question is whether you will use it.

Now that you know how to fight with truth, it is time to learn how

Chapter 6: The Weapons

to speak it through prayer. The next weapon is not only how you communicate with God, but how God moves on your behalf.

Prayer: God's Communication Line

If the Word of God is your sword, then prayer is your lifeline. It keeps you connected to your Commander, God Himself. Prayer is not a religious routine. It is the weapon that turns fear into faith and weakness into strength. Prayer is not about persuading God to do your will, but about learning to trust what He wills to do in and through you, according to His purpose (Romans 8:28).

"...*The effectual fervent prayer of a righteous man availeth much*" (James 5:16). Notice that word *"effectual."* Not casual prayer, not occasional prayer, but fervent prayer. A prayer life that engages the heart of God will soon engage His hand, His power in action. Prayer is not about getting God's attention. It's about giving Him yours.

Prayer is not a ritual.
It is a lifeline.

There have been seasons in my life when prayer felt like the only thing holding me together. I didn't have answers, but I had access, to God Himself. That access reminded me that even when life felt out of control, my God never was. Prayer steadies the heart because it shifts your focus from what you cannot do to what God can already do. In prayer, peace often arrives before the answer does.

When Babylon changed Daniel's language, his name, and his surroundings, it never changed his habit. He prayed. "*Now when Daniel knew that the writing was signed, he went into his house; and his windows being open in his chamber toward Jerusalem, he kneeled upon his knees three times a day, and prayed, and gave thanks before his God, as he did aforetime*" (Daniel 6:10). Daniel did not begin praying when things went wrong. He had already been praying when everything seemed right. That consistency became his shield. When they threw him into the lions' den, he did not panic. He continued what he had always practiced.

Spiritual Warfare: Building Your Battle Plan

The early church followed that same pattern. When Peter was imprisoned, the believers did not organize a protest. They gathered for prayer. *"Peter therefore was kept in prison: but prayer was made without ceasing of the church unto God for him"* (Acts 12:5). They prayed through the night, and God sent an angel to open the prison doors. That was not coincidence. It was divine power. When the church prays, God moves in accordance with His will and promises (1 John 5:14).

Prayer is not learned in crisis.
It is tested and proven there.

I've seen it in our church too. There was a season when a family faced overwhelming medical news. The doctors had no good options. The outlook was dark. But the church gathered, laid hands on them, and prayed with one accord. We didn't demand God do what we wanted. We submitted to His will and asked for His strength. The situation didn't change overnight, but peace flooded that home. Strength returned. And in time, God brought healing in ways the doctors couldn't explain. Prayer didn't just change the outcome. It changed the family.

That's what prayer does. It keeps the line open between the battlefield and the throne room.

Prayer has two sides: discipline and direction. The discipline of prayer is your daily connection. The direction of prayer is your Spirit-led response in battle. Every believer needs both. Daily prayer builds strength before the fight. Battle prayer applies that strength during the fight. The disciplined life of prayer fills the heart with peace. The directed prayer of battle releases power. Together, they keep you from reacting in fear.

The most powerful prayers are not creative. They are scriptural. Jesus said, *"If ye abide in me, and my words abide in you, ye shall ask what ye will, and it shall be done unto you"* (John 15:7). Prayer and the Word are inseparable. The Word gives prayer its direction. Obedient prayer displays the power of the Word already proven true (Hebrews 4:12). When you pray the Word, you are praying God's will. When you pray His promises, you are claiming ground already secured

Chapter 6: The Weapons

by His power.

That is why prayer is not emotional. It is positional, rooted in your standing in Christ, not in your feelings. It does not depend on how you feel but on where you stand, in faith, resting in your position in Christ as a child of God (Ephesians 2:6).

There will be times when answers seem delayed and silence feels heavy. But delay is not denial. Elijah prayed seven times before the cloud appeared. Daniel prayed twenty-one days before the angel arrived. Persistence in prayer is proof of faith, not weakness, because faith keeps believing even when there's no visible answer. God is never late. He is always aligning circumstances to His perfect timing. And while you wait, prayer keeps your heart in step with His timing.

I have learned that sometimes the greatest answers come after the longest silence. Those waiting moments in prayer are never wasted. They are where trust is forged. God may not change your situation right away, but He will always change you through it. The longer the waiting, the deeper the work He is doing within.

Prayer keeps you connected to God's command.

A soldier who stops communicating with his Commander soon fights in confusion. Prayer keeps your orders clear and your heart steady. It reminds you who leads, who fights, and who wins. Develop the discipline of daily communication with God. Start small if you must, even five minutes in the Word and five minutes in prayer, but be consistent.

The power of prayer is not in its length, but in the life that flows through it. *"Call unto me, and I will answer thee, and show thee great and mighty things, which thou knowest not"* (Jeremiah 33:3). When you call, God answers. That is not poetry. It is promise.

Prayer keeps you connected to God's command, but there is another weapon that brings His presence into the battlefield, praise. When you learn to praise before you see victory, you learn how to fight with joy.

Praise: Worship as Warfare

Every soldier knows that morale can win or lose a battle. In spiritual warfare, praise is that morale. It strengthens faith, steadies the heart, and shifts your focus from the strength of the enemy to the greatness of God. *"And when they began to sing and to praise, the LORD set ambushments against the children of Ammon, Moab, and mount Seir, which were come against Judah; and they were smitten"* (2 Chronicles 20:22).

Praise is worship expressed in the middle of battle, a weapon of faith that exalts God above the fight. It is the sound of faith before the answer is seen, and the language of trust before triumph. Fear magnifies problems, but praise magnifies God. When you praise, the battle may not disappear, yet its size changes. The enemy may still surround you, but your heart begins to see the Lord standing larger than the opposition.

"In every thing give thanks: for this is the will of God in Christ Jesus concerning you" (1 Thessalonians 5:18). Thanksgiving keeps you from sinking into discouragement. Praise is not denial of reality. It is declaration of God's authority. It does not ignore the problem. It reminds the problem of Who rules over it.

When three armies marched toward Judah, King Jehoshaphat did not call for generals first. He called for singers. *"And when he had consulted with the people, he appointed singers unto the Lord, and that should praise the beauty of holiness, as they went out before the army"* (2 Chronicles 20:21). They praised before the battle was won because their praise placed trust fully in God's power to fight for them, and victory came in the middle of their worship. The Lord fought while they sang.

Praise strengthens faith, confounds the enemy, and fills the heart with expectation instead of fear.

Praise in pain often feels unnatural. Your emotions resist it, your circumstances do not justify it, and your mind argues against it. Yet something happens when you lift your voice anyway. The weight begins to lift, peace replaces panic, and what felt heavy starts to feel holy. Praise may not change circumstances immediately, but it changes something within you first.

Chapter 6: The Weapons

I've seen this in our church. There was a season when a family faced deep grief after losing a loved one. The pain was raw, the questions many. But in the middle of it, they chose praise. They came to service, lifted their hands, and sang even through tears. It wasn't loud or dramatic. It was quiet obedience. But week by week, peace grew. Joy returned in measures they didn't expect. Praise didn't erase the loss, but it carried them through it.

Praise may not change circumstances immediately, but it changes something within you first.

The story of Paul and Silas offers another glimpse of this power. *"And at midnight Paul and Silas prayed, and sang praises unto God: and the prisoners heard them. And suddenly there was a great earthquake"* (Acts 16:25–26). Their backs were bleeding, their feet chained, and the prison walls pressed close, but their praise broke what pain built. Chains fell, doors opened, and fear turned into freedom. Their song was not for escape. It was for God's glory. Praise lifted them above the circumstance until Heaven shook the earth.

Praise is not a feeling to wait for. It is a choice to make. Worship does not begin with music. It begins with memory, remembering what God has done. When you remember, gratitude rises and faith grows. In the morning, praise Him for new mercy. At noon, praise Him for strength. At night, praise Him for His faithfulness. Start small, speak sincerely, and watch the heaviness lift.

"But thou art holy, O thou that inhabitest the praises of Israel" (Psalm 22:3). When you praise, you become aware of God's presence that already fills the space, and where His presence is acknowledged, fear cannot remain (Psalm 139:7–10). Thanksgiving disarms the enemy because it refuses to complain. The devil cannot operate in a grateful heart. His accusations lose power where worship breathes.

A thankful believer is an unshakable believer.

Gratitude guards the mind, softens the spirit, and turns trials into testimonies (Philippians 4:11–13; 1 Thessalonians 5:18).

Spiritual Warfare: Building Your Battle Plan

"*Enter into his gates with thanksgiving, and into his courts with praise: be thankful unto him, and bless his name*" (Psalm 100:4). Every time you praise in pain, you strike a blow against darkness. Every time you thank God in trial, you declare His sovereignty again. Lift your voice when fear tells you to be silent. Praise before you see change, and peace will replace panic.

There have been times I have praised God through tears, not because I felt victorious but because I knew He was worthy. Those moments did not erase the battle, but they reminded me I was not fighting alone. Praise builds altars, moments of surrender and remembrance, in the middle of ashes and teaches the heart to trust while waiting.

"*Let every thing that hath breath praise the LORD. Praise ye the LORD*" (Psalm 150:6). Praise steadies the heart and fills the atmosphere with faith.

There is another weapon that makes the enemy flee, the authority of Jesus' Name. Let us now learn how to stand and speak under His command.

The Name and Authority of Jesus Christ

Every army operates by authority. A private may carry the same weapon as a general, but without authority, he carries no command or backing. In the same way, you carry spiritual power as a believer, but that power only flows when you're submitted to Christ's authority.

"*Submit yourselves therefore to God. Resist the devil, and he will flee from you.*" (James 4:7) Notice the order: submit first, then resist. Submission comes before strength. You who are out of alignment with Heaven can't expect victory on earth.

When you stand in Christ's Name, you stand under His rule.

Authority doesn't begin with you. It flows through you when you're surrendered to Christ. Jesus said, "*Behold, I give unto you power to tread on serpents and scorpions, and over all the power of the enemy: and nothing shall by any means hurt you*" (Luke 10:19).

Chapter 6: The Weapons

That word power speaks of delegated authority, strength that is borrowed, not self-made.

You are not speaking on your own behalf. You are speaking under His authority, as His representative (2 Corinthians 5:20). That is why the devil does not fear your name. He fears the Name you stand under.

When Peter and John met the lame man at the temple gate, Peter did not offer charity. He offered authority. *"Then Peter said, Silver and gold have I none; but such as I have give I thee: In the name of Jesus Christ of Nazareth rise up and walk"* (Acts 3:6). That moment was not about Peter's ability. It was about Jesus' authority. The same Name that raised the dead still raises the broken. The same power that healed that man still works through every believer who walks in obedience and faith.

I remember the first time this truth became real to me. I was praying over a situation that felt impossible, fear pressing in, confusion swirling, resistance rising on every side. But as I prayed in Jesus' Name, not as a phrase, but as a position, everything shifted. The pressure lifted, peace entered, and strength returned. It wasn't my words that made the difference. It was His authority covering me as I prayed.

When fear presses in, pray in His Name. When spiritual pressure builds, speak in His Name. When confusion clouds your thoughts, declare His Name. Your authority is not found in shouting at darkness but in standing under the Light, living under Christ's authority.

To use His Name rightly is to remember: you are not the commander. You are the commissioned.

Every victory you will ever win begins at the cross, where His death and resurrection secured eternal triumph once for all (Colossians 2:15; 1 Corinthians 15:57).

"Wherefore God also hath highly exalted him, and given him a name which is above every name: That at the name of Jesus every knee should bow, of things in heaven, and things in earth, and things under the earth" (Philippians 2:9–10). That is not a metaphor. It is a mandate. Hell still bows to that Name.

To walk in authority, you must walk in humility. The believer who stays under command never has to fear the fight. When your life aligns with God's order, the Name of Jesus becomes more than a word. It becomes a weapon. Speak it with reverence, stand in it with confidence, and trust in it with your life.

"*The name of the LORD is a strong tower: the righteous runneth into it, and is safe*" (Proverbs 18:10). The believer who stays under command never has to fear the fight.

You have now learned to fight with truth, prayer, praise, and authority. But there is still one weapon that makes the enemy flee, the blood of Christ and the word of your testimony.

The Blood of Christ and the Word of Our Testimony

Every believer fights two battles. One is against the enemy's lies from the outside, and the other is the weight of guilt and shame from the inside. The blood of Christ is the weapon that settles both.

"*And they overcame him by the blood of the Lamb, and by the word of their testimony; and they loved not their lives unto the death*" (Revelation 12:11). The cross isn't just a symbol of forgiveness. It's the declaration of victory. The blood speaks when accusation rises. It silences the enemy's voice and strengthens your heart. From Genesis to Revelation, the blood marks the path of redemption. In Egypt, it was placed on the doorposts for protection. At Calvary, it was poured out for salvation. Every drop testifies that sin has been paid for and that the accuser has lost his case, his right to condemn you.

"*In whom we have redemption through his blood, even the forgiveness of sins*" (Colossians 1:14). The blood of Christ doesn't simply cover sin. It cleanses it. It removes guilt, erases condemnation, and restores fellowship with God. It is your assurance that no accusation can stand where the blood has been applied.

The blood of Christ doesn't cover sin.
The blood of Christ conquers it.

I've walked with believers who knew the verses about forgiveness but still carried old shame like a backpack. They'd say, "*Pastor, I know God forgave me, but I can't let it go.*" One man in our church had fallen years earlier, and even after confession, the enemy kept bringing it up. Every time he tried to serve, the whisper came: "*You're disqualified.*"

Chapter 6: The Weapons

We sat down, opened Romans 8, and read *"There is therefore now no condemnation to them which are in Christ Jesus"* (Romans 8:1). That truth hit him like fresh air. He said, *"It's like the weight finally lifted."* The blood had already done the work. He just needed to believe it.

A testimony is not a performance. It's proof that God's grace is still working in your life. It's your living declaration that the same blood that saved you now sustains you. When you share your testimony, you're not boasting. You're bearing witness to victory. Every time you tell how God delivered you, you strike a blow against the enemy's deception.

"Let the redeemed of the LORD say so, whom he hath redeemed from the hand of the enemy" (Psalm 107:2). The enemy's goal is to keep you silent because silence hides victory. Testimony turns confession of faith into courage. It reminds others, and yourself, that the power of Christ still works today.

Peter's life shows this perfectly. He knew the sting of failure and the weight of denial. Yet after the resurrection, Jesus met him on the shore, restored him, and called him again to follow. The same man who once swore he did not know Christ stood boldly at Pentecost proclaiming His Name before thousands. What changed was not Peter's personality. It was his heart, cleansed and restored by grace. The blood had cleansed him, and his testimony became his weapon.

Many believers love God but still live chained to regret. The blood of Christ breaks those chains, and your testimony keeps them from returning. It reminds you and others of the truth that set you free. When guilt attacks your peace, rest in the blood of Christ and declare its power over sin and condemnation (Romans 5:9; Hebrews 9:14). When shame whispers lies, speak your testimony. The blood reminds you of what God has done. Your testimony reminds you of what He is still doing.

You can confidently declare, *"I am forgiven. I am redeemed. I am free."* These are not slogans. They are affirmations of faith grounded in the finished work of the cross (Galatians 6:14; 1 Corinthians 1:18).

"There is therefore now no condemnation to them which are in Christ Jesus" (Romans 8:1). The enemy cannot argue with what Christ has finished. Do not let your past write your story when the blood has already written your freedom. Do not let guilt keep you quiet when

grace has given you a voice. Speak your testimony boldly. Every time you do, you remind the devil of his defeat and your deliverance.

"*Having therefore, brethren, boldness to enter into the holiest by the blood of Jesus*" (Hebrews 10:19). You have access. You have acceptance. You have assurance. That is what the blood secured and what your testimony declares.

The blood of Christ settles every accusation, and your testimony reinforces every truth. But to stay free, the believer must stay clean. The next weapon closes the doors the enemy tries to reopen, confession and repentance.

Confession and Repentance: Closing the Enemy's Doors

The enemy cannot steal what Christ has secured, but he will always look for an open door, an unconfessed sin or lingering compromise. Confession and repentance are how you shut that door firmly, quickly, and completely. "*If we confess our sins, he is faithful and just to forgive us our sins, and to cleanse us from all unrighteousness*" (1 John 1:9).

Confession is not a ritual. It is a return to fellowship. Repentance is not punishment. It is protection. These are not weapons of shame but shields of restoration. Pride keeps doors open, but humility closes them.

"*He that covereth his sins shall not prosper: but whoso confesseth and forsaketh them shall have mercy*" (Proverbs 28:13).

When you sin, the Spirit convicts not to condemn you, but to call you home. Confession brings the soul into the light where darkness loses its grip. You cannot overcome what you continue to hide. When sin is exposed before God, it is expelled from the enemy's reach. Regular confession keeps your fellowship sincere and your spirit free.

I have learned that the longer you carry unconfessed sin, the heavier it becomes. Prayer feels forced, praise feels distant, and your thoughts drift more toward what you have done instead of Who God is. But the moment you bring your sin into the light, freedom comes rushing in. God's forgiveness is instant and complete, but too often you delay confession as if He will love you more when you have felt sorry long enough. He does not need your delay. He desires your

Chapter 6: The Weapons

return.

Repentance is more than saying *"I'm sorry."* It is a change of direction, turning away from sin and returning to the Savior. The prodigal son did not just regret the far country. He rose and went home. That is repentance in motion. When you repent, you trade distance for closeness, guilt for grace, and failure for freedom. It is how spiritual momentum is restored after a stumble.

"Draw nigh to God, and he will draw nigh to you." (James 4:8) David's story gives you a powerful picture of both the danger of silence and the beauty of confession. The same man who conquered Goliath later fell to temptation. When he tried to hide his sin, he wrote, *"When I kept silence, my bones waxed old through my roaring all the day long"* (Psalm 32:3). But when he confessed, peace returned: *"I acknowledged my sin unto thee, and mine iniquity have I not hid... and thou forgavest the iniquity of my sin"* (Psalm 32:5). Confession turned misery into mercy. That is what happens when the heart returns to God.

Make confession part of your prayer life, not just your rescue. Search your heart daily and respond quickly when conviction comes. I often pray, *"Lord, show me anything that grieves You."* That simple request has spared me from many wrong turns. When He brings something to light, call it what it is, forsake it, and replace it with truth. Sin grows in silence, but it loses its grip in honesty.

When you confess, God restores fellowship instantly and completely, for your forgiveness was already secured at Calvary (1 John 1:9; Hebrews 10:17–18). He does not put you on probation. He restores you to fellowship. *"As far as the east is from the west, so far hath he removed our transgressions from us"* (Psalm 103:12).

Grace does not make sin smaller. It makes salvation stronger. Sin tolerated today becomes bondage tomorrow. Deal with it quickly, and the door stays closed. Keep your heart tender and your conscience clear.

"Create in me a clean heart, O God; and renew a right spirit within me" (Psalm 51:10). A clean heart is a ready heart, and a ready heart is a victorious one.

Confession keeps the heart clean, but fasting sharpens the spirit. The next weapon teaches you how surrender becomes strength.

Spiritual Warfare: Building Your Battle Plan

Fasting: Strength Through Surrender

Fasting is one of the most misunderstood weapons in your arsenal. Many see it as punishment for the body, but in truth, it is training for the soul. Fasting does not twist God's arm. It trains your heart. "*Is not this the fast that I have chosen? to loose the bands of wickedness, to undo the heavy burdens, and to let the oppressed go free, and that ye break every yoke?*" (Isaiah 58:6).

Fasting weakens the hold of the flesh so faith can grow. It quiets the noise of the world so the voice of God can be heard. When the flesh is denied, the spirit is sharpened. In a world overflowing with distraction, fasting cuts through the clutter. It clears the heart and refocuses the soul.

Jesus said, "*Moreover when ye fast, be not, as the hypocrites, of a sad countenance... But thou, when thou fastest, anoint thine head, and wash thy face; That thou appear not unto men to fast, but unto thy Father which is in secret: and thy Father, which seeth in secret, shall reward thee openly*" (Matthew 6:16–18). Notice that Jesus said when you fast, not if. He assumed His followers would fast, not to be seen by others, but to be strengthened by God. Fasting is not about public proof. It is about private strength in God's presence. What happens in secret between you and God soon bears fruit in the open.

Fasting does not get God's attention. It gives Him yours.

Before Jesus began His public ministry, He fasted forty days in the wilderness. At His weakest physical moment, He stood strongest in spirit. Fasting did not make Him divine. It revealed His dependence as the Son of Man. It showed that spiritual victory begins with spiritual surrender. The devil tempted Him with appetite, ambition, and authority, but every temptation fell before the same response: "*...It is written...*" (Matthew 4:4, 7, 10). Fasting and the Word together form an unbreakable defense.

I've counseled believers who thought fasting was about endurance, how long they could go without food. But I've learned it's less about what you give up and more about what you gain. It's not a

Chapter 6: The Weapons

hunger strike. It's a heart posture. You learn quickly that fasting clears the fog from your faith and reminds you that you depend on God for every breath, every step, every need.

Fasting is not an act of deprivation but an expression of devotion. When the heart humbles itself before God, fasting becomes a language of longing that says, *"Lord, I want You more than what sustains me."* Jesus declared, *"...Man shall not live by bread alone, but by every word that proceedeth out of the mouth of God"* (Matthew 4:4).

The goal of fasting is not emptiness but exchange, trading the temporary for the eternal.

Start simple. Fast from one meal, one day, or even from distractions, anything that dulls your awareness of God's presence. Every fast should include three things:

1. Purpose: *Know why you are fasting.*
2. Plan: *Know how and for how long.*
3. Posture: *Approach it with humility before God.*

Use that time to pray, read the Word, and listen. After Jesus fasted, *"...Jesus returned in the power of the Spirit into Galilee"* (Luke 4:14). That was not coincidence. It was consequence. Fasting restores alignment with God's will, and that alignment allows His authority to work unhindered through a surrendered heart (2 Corinthians 12:9; John 15:5). When the heart is right, you become a vessel through whom God's power can freely work (2 Timothy 2:21). When the flesh is subdued, faith becomes strong.

"Humble yourselves therefore under the mighty hand of God, that he may exalt you in due time" (1 Peter 5:6). Humility always precedes honor. Fasting is not proof of devotion. It is pursuit of direction, seeking clarity from God. You are not trying to get God to move. You are moving closer to Him.

Every moment you turn from the world's noise, you turn toward Heaven's voice.

Spiritual Warfare: Building Your Battle Plan

Fasting draws you closer to God, but no believer was meant to fight alone. The next weapon reminds us that unity is strength, agreement and accountability keep soldiers standing.

Agreement and Accountability: Fighting Together

One of the enemy's oldest tricks is isolation. He wants you to believe no one will understand, no one will care, and no one can help. But that's a lie designed to keep you alone and defenseless. *"Two are better than one; because they have a good reward for their labour. For if they fall, the one will lift up his fellow"* (Ecclesiastes 4:9–10). Every soldier in battle needs a comrade, and every believer in warfare needs a brother or sister in Christ who will stand beside them.

When you're under attack, pride whispers, *"You can handle it yourself."* But independence is not true strength. It's self-reliance disguised as strength. God designed His people for fellowship. When Moses' arms grew weary on the hill, Aaron and Hur held them up until the battle was won (Exodus 17:11–12). That's the power of partnership in spiritual warfare.

Sometimes victory doesn't come through another sermon. It comes through another believer praying with you. Sometimes what you need most is not advice but companionship, someone's steady presence that reminds you you're not alone. This is why church matters. The local church isn't just a place to attend. It is the army God assembled for your protection. When you isolate yourself, you walk away from your reinforcements.

"Not forsaking the assembling of ourselves together, but exhorting one another" (Hebrews 10:25). The word exhorting means encouraging and strengthening. That's what happens when believers gather. The Spirit of God works through the fellowship of the saints to build courage and renew resolve (Philippians 2:1–2; Acts 2:42).

You're not meant to fight alone.
God gave you the church for a reason.

I've seen it countless times in our church. A weary believer finds renewed strength simply by sharing their battle with someone godly.

Chapter 6: The Weapons

It wasn't fancy counseling or deep insight. It was the simple power of prayer and presence. If you're in a fight, don't face it alone. Find a trusted Christian who knows the Word and walks with God. Ask them to pray with you and hold you accountable. That one humble step can close the door of isolation and open the door of victory.

Obedience: The Ultimate Weapon

Every spiritual weapon God provides finds its strength in one thing, obedience. Without it, truth is learned but not lived, prayer is spoken but not believed, and power is claimed but never demonstrated. Obedience is not the final weapon because it is least. It is final because it holds all the others together.

"*...To obey is better than sacrifice, and to hearken than the fat of rams*" (1 Samuel 15:22). Disobedience cost Saul his crown. Obedience gave David his victories. God honors those who trust Him enough to do what He says. Obedience is faith wearing boots, faith that moves forward even when the outcome is unseen. It does not always make sense, but it always leads to victory.

"*But be ye doers of the word, and not hearers only, deceiving your own selves*" (James 1:22). You cannot claim victory while ignoring the orders of God's Word. When you obey the Word, you align your life with the will of God, and that alignment is victory itself. Every act of obedience declares that God's wisdom is greater than human reasoning.

Peter learned this truth by the water's edge. After a long and fruitless night of fishing, Jesus told him to cast the net one more time. Peter could have argued, he was the fisherman, and Jesus was the carpenter, but instead, he obeyed. "*...Master, we have toiled all the night, and have taken nothing: nevertheless at thy word I will let down the net*" (Luke 5:5). One simple act of obedience turned failure into fullness. The nets broke, the boat overflowed, and Peter fell to his knees in awe. That is the power of obedience. It transforms empty effort into divine encounter.

Abraham's story teaches the same lesson in a deeper way. When God called him to offer Isaac, obedience walked him up the mountain while faith whispered, "*God will provide.*" Scripture says, "*By faith*

Spiritual Warfare: Building Your Battle Plan

Abraham, when he was tried, offered up Isaac" (Hebrews 11:17). Abraham's obedience did not merely prove his love. It revealed God's provision. Every step of obedience carries revelation on the other side.

Obedience is not a single act. It is a lifestyle. It shows up in the quiet decisions before it shines in the public victories. It is how you respond when conviction comes, how you treat others when no one is watching, and how you live truth when it challenges your comfort. Every *"yes"* to God strengthens your armor. Every delayed obedience weakens it.

"Trust in the LORD with all thine heart; and lean not unto thine own understanding. In all thy ways acknowledge him, and he shall direct thy paths" (Proverbs 3:5–6). Obedience does not always feel powerful in the moment, but it always positions you for God's best. It does not make you strong. It makes you unstoppable, because it keeps you under God's strength and command. *"If ye be willing and obedient, ye shall eat the good of the land"* (Isaiah 1:19).

Obedience does not earn blessing. It positions you to receive what God in grace already desires to give (James 1:17; Ephesians 2:8–10).

Every victory in Scripture began with obedience.

Whether Jericho's walls falling, seas parting, or giants collapsing, the pattern was the same: the command came, the people responded, and God acted. That truth has never changed. When you say yes to God, He works through your obedience to accomplish His will and show His power (Philippians 2:13).

Every time you obey, the enemy loses ground. Every time you delay, he gains ground. Do not wait for perfect conditions. Obey in faith, and God will make a way. Your obedience is the loudest *"Yes"* to God and the strongest *"No"* to Satan.

"Submit yourselves therefore to God. Resist the devil, and he will flee from you" (James 4:7). Submission is obedience in action, and resistance is its reward. When you stand under God's command, the enemy has no choice but to retreat. Obedience brings every weapon together and prepares you to stand fully armed and fully guarded.

You have learned how to fight. Now it is time to be protected while

Chapter 6: The Weapons

you fight, as Ephesians 6 teaches. Weapons win battles, but armor sustains warriors. The next chapter will teach you how to wear that armor with strength and confidence.

Obedience binds all the weapons of faith into one victorious life.

6

BUILD YOUR BATTLE PLAN

THE WEAPONS

You now know the weapons God has placed in your hands. But possession alone does not mean victory. A weapon unused, misused, or deployed at the wrong moment leaves a soldier exposed. Many believers lose ground not because they lack truth, prayer, or authority, but because they have never learned how to wield those weapons during the fight.

Spiritual victory is not accidental. It is practiced and then learned. It is forged through disciplined obedience, knowing which weapon to use, when to use it, and how to hold your ground without hesitation.

Purpose of This Battle Plan

The purpose of this battle plan is to train you to deploy God's weapons intentionally and in order when the spiritual attack begins.

This plan is designed to help you:
- Select the right weapon for the right moment.
- Respond to an attack with obedience rather than reaction.
- Keep the enemy from reclaiming ground you already won.
- Establish a consistent rhythm of victory through disciplined use of God's provision.

Step 1: Select Your Primary Weapons

Not every battle requires every weapon at once. A soldier who reaches for everything often uses nothing well. Victory comes from discernment, knowing where the enemy is attacking and responding with the right weapons God has already provided.

How to do it?

Before you move forward, identify where the attack is strongest *right now*, then intentionally select *two primary weapons* to answer that attack.

Choose according to the area under attack:

1. **Mental Attack**
   (fear, anxiety, intrusive thoughts, confusion, discouragement)

   Primary Weapons:
   - *The Word of God*
   - *Prayer*

   Why This Works:

   Mental battles are not won by willpower. They are won when truth replaces lies and prayer brings the mind back under God's authority. Scripture exposes deception, and prayer restores clarity and peace.

2. **Spiritual Attack**
   (temptation, guilt, shame, accusation, distance from God)

   Primary Weapons:
   - The Blood of Christ
   - Confession and Repentance

   Why This Works:
   Spiritual attacks thrive on accusation and compromise. They gain strength when guilt lingers. The blood of Jesus silences every accusation and strips condemnation of its authority. Repentance closes the door, cuts off the enemy's access, and restores clear fellowship with God.

3. **Physical Attack**
   (fatigue, illness, weakness, burnout)

   Primary Weapons:
   - Prayer
   - Praise

   Why This Works:
   Physical weakness amplifies fear and discouragement. When the body is depleted, the enemy's voice sounds louder and resistance feels harder. Prayer draws strength directly from God, renewing both the body and resolve. Praise lifts the soul and reorients focus toward God's power.

4. **Financial Attack**
   (fear of provision, anxiety, instability, pressure)

   Primary Weapons:
   - The Word of God
   - Obedience

Why This Works:

Financial attacks target trust. They provoke worry, invite shortcuts, and push toward panic. Scripture anchors the heart in God's promises and reasserts Him as the true Provider. Obedience keeps your steps aligned with His direction instead of chasing desperate solutions.

5. **Relational Attack**
   (conflict, isolation, bitterness, division)

   ### Primary Weapons:
   - Prayer
   - Agreement and Accountability

   ### Why This Works:

   Relational warfare thrives on isolation. It distorts emotion and fuels division. Prayer guards the heart and exposes the lies at work. Godly accountability secures clarity and keeps emotion from taking control.

Now It's Your Turn:

Write the two weapons you are selecting for this battle:

Weapon 1: _____

Weapon 2: _____

A Word of Clarity About Your Weapons

Choosing primary weapons does not mean abandoning the others. Every weapon God has given you remains necessary. The distinction is not value, but timing. In each battle, certain weapons must be engaged first while others remain in position.

Think in terms of primary and supporting weapons. Primary weapons confront the immediate attack. Supporting weapons reinforce, protect, and help you hold the ground you have taken.

All of God's Weapons Remain Active

Even as you focus on your two primary weapons, the following must continue to shape your daily walk:

- The Word of God
- Praise
- Prayer
- Fasting
- Obedience
- Confession and Repentance
- Agreement and Accountability
- The Name and Authority of Jesus Christ
- The Blood of Christ and Your Testimony

These weapons work together. Neglecting one weakens the whole. But when they are used in harmony, the believer stands equipped, guarded, and ready.

Step 2: Deploy The Weapons In Obedience

Choosing your weapons is only the beginning. Victory comes through use, not possession. A weapon carried but not deployed offers no protection.

Many believers know what to do but hesitate once the fight is underway. That hesitation gives the enemy room to advance and apply greater pressure.

This step is about action, not analysis.

How to Do It?

Take the two primary weapons you selected in **Step 1** and use them intentionally, not emotionally. Do not wait for the attack to pass. Do not wait until you *"feel ready."* Authority is exercised through obedience, not readiness.

- If your weapon is the **Word of God**, speak Scripture aloud. *Do not paraphrase. Declare what God has already said.*

- If your weapon is **Praise**, praise God before circumstances change. *Praise shifts the battleground before the outcome appears.*

- If your weapon is **Prayer**, pray immediately and directly. *Do not fear. Bring the situation under God's authority.*

- If your weapon is **Fasting** deny the flesh to strengthen the spirit. *Set the time and purpose, then replace appetite with prayer and the Word.*

- If your weapon is **Obedience**, act on what God has already made clear. Obedience delayed is ground surrendered.

- If your weapon is **Confession and Repentance**, confess quickly and turn decisively. *Do not negotiate with conviction.*

- If your weapon is **Agreement and Accountability**, involve another believer immediately. *Isolation strengthens the enemy's position.*

- If your weapon is **The Name and Authority of Jesus Christ,** submit to God and speak in His Name. *Do not argue with the enemy. Stand under Christ's authority and resist.*

- If your weapon is **The Blood of Christ and Your Testimony**, declare what the blood has finished. *Refuse accusation. Speak forgiveness, freedom, and redemption without hesitation.*

Now It's Your Turn:

Use the two primary weapons you selected in **Step 1** immediately.

Write one clear sentence describing how you will deploy each weapon. *Be specific. Do not write intentions. Write actions.*

Weapon 1 Deployment:

"When the attack comes, I will

_____."

Weapon 2 Deployment:

"When the attack comes, I will

_____."

Do it once right now.

- If your weapon involves Scripture, read it aloud.
- If it involves prayer, pray it now.
- If it involves confession, confess it now.
- If it involves obedience, take the first step today.

Step 3: Hold The Ground

Winning a battle is not the same as winning the war. The enemy often retreats temporarily, only to return and test whether the battleground is guarded. This step prevents relapse, retreat, and spiritual drift.

The very second you assume the fight is finished and drop your guard, the enemy will probe for weakness and attempt to retake what was lost. Now is not the time to relax. Now is the time to fortify.

How to Do It?

- Continue using your primary weapons daily.
- Maintain the supporting weapons active.
- Reject every lie that has already been exposed.
- Do not reopen doors you have already closed.

The enemy does not retake ground through strength. He retakes it through neglect. Whatever you stop practicing, you surrender back to him.

- Guard your routines.
- Guard your thinking.
- Guard your obedience.

Now It's Your Turn:

Holding ground requires intention. Decide now how you will prevent retreat.

1. Identify one practice you must maintain.
This is not a new discipline. It is one you already know you need.

"I will guard this ground by continuing to _____

_____."

2. **Identify something that would reopen the door.**

   "I will refuse to return to _____

   _____.*"*

3. **Choose someone who will help keep you accountable.**

   "This ground will be guarded with the help of _____

   _____.*"*

7

THE ARMOR

Before the battle begins,
you must put on the armor.

You've learned how to fight with the weapons God gave you. You've seen how truth cuts through lies, how prayer brings heaven's power, how praise shifts the atmosphere, how authority breaks chains. But weapons win battles. Armor keeps the warrior standing long enough to see the victory.

God never sends His children into war unequipped. He arms you with truth, prayer, praise, and authority. And He covers you with His grace. Every weapon we studied has one purpose: to prepare you not just to fight, but to stand. When the dust settles and the smoke clears, the believer who stands in obedience and faith will still be there, firm in Christ.

"Wherefore take unto you the whole armour of God, that ye may be able to withstand in the evil day, and having done all, to stand" (Ephesians 6:13). Standing isn't passive. It's power held firm, like a soldier braced against the charge. The enemy may press hard, but he can't prevail when you stand in the Lord's strength. You're not standing on your own ground. You're standing on the victory Christ

Spiritual Warfare: Building Your Battle Plan

already won. His death and resurrection conquered sin and death once for all. *"But thanks be to God, which giveth us the victory through our Lord Jesus Christ"* (1 Corinthians 15:57). The armor makes sure you endure every skirmish until the end.

I've seen believers who know how to fight but forget how to stand. They swing the sword well in a crisis, but they grow weary when the battle drags on. God calls you to both, to battle with courage and to stand with conviction. The battle may rage, but the soldier who stands under God's protection will not waver.

I once watched a faithful woman in our church walk through months of sickness. Her body weakened, but her Bible stayed open beside the bed. Her voice grew faint, but Scripture still passed her lips like quiet marching orders from Heaven. There were no more shouts of victory, only the steady whisper of trust. Each time I visited, she smiled and said, *"I'm still standing in Christ,"* still trusting Christ to hold her upright. That is the posture of victory, not movement, but endurance. Not noise, but faith that refuses to fall.

The goal of spiritual warfare isn't only to fight. It's to remain standing.

This is where training meets the test. You've learned how to fight with truth and prayer, how to lift praise in pain, how to walk in authority, how to live in obedience. Now it's time to hold your ground when the fight comes to you.

Ephesians 6 shows the armor as both protection and proclamation. Each piece declares who you are in Christ. You're not standing in fear. You're standing in faith. Not holding on to survive, but standing firm to testify that your God reigns.

"Finally, my brethren, be strong in the Lord, and in the power of his might" (Ephesians 6:10). God has given you everything you need to win, not only the weapons to fight, but the armor to remain unshaken.

You're not only armed.
You're prepared to stand!

Chapter 7: The Armor

The Call to Stand

The call to stand isn't a call to stillness. It's a call to readiness. Standing is strength under God's command, the quiet determination of a soldier awaiting orders.

Standing begins long before you strike the enemy's first blow. We often imagine victory as motion, swinging, running, conquering. But the Lord measures victory by endurance. When Paul wrote, *"...and having done all, to stand"* (Ephesians 6:13), he described more than defense. Standing is the spiritual posture of a heart that refuses to surrender ground already won by Christ through His finished work. *"Having spoiled principalities and powers, he made a shew of them openly, triumphing over them in it"* (Colossians 2:15).

Every soldier in God's army must learn this rhythm: readiness, resistance, and rest, a holy balance between action and dependence. Readiness prepares you to meet the enemy's advance. Resistance holds your line when pressure mounts. Rest restores you in the confidence that the Lord fights for you. Without this rhythm, warfare becomes exhaustion. With it, endurance becomes worship.

I think of a young couple I counseled who entered a season of relentless loss, job gone, health shaken, future uncertain. Their days blurred into doctor visits and unanswered prayers. Bills piled like battle reports on the table, and sleep came hard. Everything in them wanted to rush, to fight, to fix. But the Lord's word to them was simple: stand.

In prayer they learned that obedience sometimes means holding ground, trusting that God's strength is enough. They began each morning not with plans but with prayer, whispering Scripture like lifelines. Months later they told me, *"We didn't win anything new, Pastor. We just didn't lose what mattered most."* That is the victory of standing.

When Paul tells you to *"withstand in the evil day,"* he's describing the unseen battle that begins before the first visible blow. Standing is not reaction. It's preparation. You don't wait for trouble to put on strength. You abide in strength before trouble arrives. That's why Scripture calls you to *"be strong in the Lord, and in the power of his might"* (Ephesians 6:10).

Dependence comes before endurance. The believer who leans on the Lord in private will stand in public. Prayer becomes the unseen training ground. Scripture becomes the balance of the soul. Obedience becomes the stance of faith. When the enemy attacks, it's too late to wonder if the armor fits. You must already be clothed in it.

Standing is both command and comfort. It reminds you that strength is not demanded. It's supplied. The same Christ who stood silent before Pilate now stands beside every believer in battle. His power sustains the posture He commands.

So then, to stand is not resignation but readiness, faith anchored, heart steady, eyes fixed. You do not shrink back when shadows lengthen. You hold the line because the Light has already overcome the darkness. Standing is not doing nothing. It's doing the one thing that matters most: remaining unmoved in Christ. *"Having done all, to stand."*

This is the spiritual posture of victory: readiness rooted in righteousness, peace secured by faith, confidence guarded by salvation, and every breath carried in prayer. Before the first step into battle, the soldier of Christ must answer the call to stand.

> **Standing is endurance
> wrapped in worship.**

The Belt of Truth

Every soldier in Paul's day understood that the belt came first. Before a Roman soldier lifted his shield or reached for his sword, he tightened the leather belt that held his tunic and armor plates together. The belt bound the armor to the body and kept it secure when the battle pressed in. Loose armor could cost a life. A tightened belt meant readiness.

Paul begins the armor of God with this same command: *"Stand therefore, having your loins girt about with truth"* (Ephesians 6:14). Truth is the first preparation. It's not decoration. It's foundation. Christ Himself is the Truth, and His Word is the unchanging measure of all things. *"I am the way, the truth, and the life"* (John 14:6).

Chapter 7: The Armor

Without Him, everything else falls apart.

Truth keeps you from unraveling, spiritually and emotionally, when pressure comes. It fastens integrity around conviction, drawing every part of your Christian life into unity. Jesus prayed, *"Sanctify them through thy truth: thy word is truth"* (John 17:17). The Word of God doesn't simply inform you. It forms you. It pulls your thoughts, motives, and emotions into harmony with the mind of Christ.

Truth is not decoration.
It's the foundation.

I remember a season when words were said that were not true, when misunderstanding traveled faster than clarity. It felt like watching smoke spread through a room I could not enter to clear. My heart wanted to defend, to chase down every rumor, and to make truth visible by force. But the Spirit of God whispered, *"Stand in truth. I will handle the rest."*

So I stayed silent and steady, praying more than I spoke. Days turned into weeks, and then truth surfaced quietly, without argument and without applause. That moment taught me a lesson I've never forgotten:

That is the strength of the belt, quiet stability. It doesn't sparkle or draw attention, yet everything depends on it. When you fasten truth each morning by reading Scripture, confessing sin, and committing to honesty before God, you walk into a world of lies already guarded.

Truth also secures integrity. It keeps your public life and private life tied together. The enemy loves to loosen the belt, to divide what you believe from how you live. But when truth is tight around the heart, duplicity has no room to breathe.

To gird with truth is to choose stability over appearance and conviction over convenience. It is to stand with a clear conscience before God and man, even when misunderstood. Every other piece of the armor depends on this one act of faith: fastening truth first.

So before the battle begins, tighten the belt. Let the Word of God define you before the world tries to. The soldier who stands in truth will not be shaken by accusation, because his strength is fastened to something eternal.

Spiritual Warfare: Building Your Battle Plan

The Breastplate of Righteousness

In battle, no piece of armor was more vital than the breastplate. When a Roman soldier fastened it across his chest, it covered the heart, the seat of life itself. A single arrow could end the fight, but a guarded heart could face the enemy unafraid. Paul chose his imagery carefully: *"...and having on the breastplate of righteousness"* (Ephesians 6:14).

Righteousness is God's protection over your heart. It guards your affections, motives, and conscience from the enemy's most personal attacks. Without it, even the strongest warrior can fall to inward wounds, pride, guilt, compromise, or bitterness. The heart that beats for God must be shielded by the righteousness of Christ, not by the fragile armor of self-effort.

"For he hath made him to be sin for us, who knew no sin; that we might be made the righteousness of God in him" (2 Corinthians 5:21). That verse is the forge where this armor is formed. Your breastplate is not earned. It's imputed, credited to you through Christ's righteousness. It's the perfect righteousness of Christ applied to your account, received by faith alone (Romans 4:5). You're called to wear it daily and live in the power of what has already been given.

I remember counseling a young man who had fallen under accusation. He wasn't guilty of what was said, but he let the weight of it pierce his spirit. His shoulders slumped, his prayers grew short, and every whisper of doubt sounded like a verdict. He wore shame like armor, heavy and cold.

But when we opened Scripture together, light began to break through. He traced the words slowly with trembling fingers and said, *"Pastor, I've been defending myself instead of letting Christ defend me."* That moment changed him. It was as if the arrow snapped in half. He stopped fighting to prove his worth and started resting in Christ's. And peace returned to his heart.

That is the protection righteousness provides. It's both your position before God and your practice in daily life. You're made righteous in Christ, and you live righteously because of Christ. When the heart stays pure before God, the enemy's darts lose their aim. *"Keep thy heart with all diligence; for out of it are the issues of life"*

Chapter 7: The Armor

(Proverbs 4:23). To guard the heart is to guard the flow of everything else, words, attitudes, and choices.

But here lies the warning: if the breastplate loosens, sin finds an opening. A compromised heart cannot stand firm for long. Pride cracks the plate. Unconfessed sin corrodes it from within. The believer who neglects righteousness soon discovers that every blow feels heavier than before. Holiness is not optional protection. It's daily survival for those already saved.

So then, put on the breastplate every morning by confessing sin quickly and walking humbly. Thank Christ for the righteousness that covers you, and let that gratitude shape the way you speak and act. Righteousness worn in humility will never become legalism. It will shine as quiet strength.

When you stand clothed in His righteousness, accusation cannot penetrate, shame cannot linger, and fear cannot rule. Your heart beats behind armor forged at Calvary, spiritual steel that no sword can pierce.

**A guarded heart
is a grounded heart.**

The Shoes of the Gospel of Peace

Roman soldiers wore thick leather sandals studded with nails to grip the ground. Those shoes were not decorative. They were their source of stability. A soldier could not advance or hold his line without firm footing. So when Paul writes, *"And your feet shod with the preparation of the gospel of peace"* (Ephesians 6:15), he reminds you that the Christian life is not lived on shifting ground. Peace gives both footing and direction. It keeps you steady and shows you where to step.

Because you've been justified by faith, you have peace with God through our Lord Jesus Christ (Romans 5:1). The gospel of peace is what keeps you from slipping when the field turns uneven. It steadies you in confusion and propels you toward those who need Christ. In daily life, where anxiety pushes, peace anchors. Where anger divides, peace unites. *"How beautiful are the feet of them that preach the gospel of peace..."* (Romans 10:15).

Spiritual Warfare: Building Your Battle Plan

I remember visiting a believer in the aftermath of a storm that had swept through his life, job lost, family strained, future uncertain. Rain still streaked the windows of his small living room, boxes half-packed in the corner. The air felt heavy with what had been lost. Yet when he opened the door, his face was calm, his Bible open on the table beside a cooling cup of coffee. *"Pastor,"* he said quietly, *"the Lord hasn't changed."*

That moment humbled me. The life-storm had taken much, but not his peace. His circumstances had moved, but his footing had not. Peace had done what strength could not, it had held him steady.

That is what it means to wear the gospel as shoes. You walk through chaos without losing direction because peace is not the absence of trouble. It's the presence of Christ, who steadies every step. When you believe the gospel deeply, peace becomes your natural ground. You step with confidence because you know who goes before you.

The soldier who forgets his shoes may run fast but not far. The believer who neglects peace may know truth and righteousness, yet still stumble in haste or reaction. Every morning, lace up your heart with the gospel again, reminding yourself that you're reconciled to God and therefore can walk reconciled before others.

"And the peace of God, which passeth all understanding, shall keep your hearts and minds through Christ Jesus" (Philippians 4:7). Peace also keeps you ready for service. The feet that carry good news are not weighed down by offense or fear. They move freely because forgiveness has lightened the load. When peace rules the heart, even hard paths feel steady underfoot.

So then, walk in the readiness of peace. The world may tremble, but the ground beneath the believer is sure. The same Lord who calmed the storm now guides every step. If you let His gospel prepare your feet, no path will be too rough, and no journey too long.

**The gospel gives peace beneath your feet
and courage within your heart.**

Chapter 7: The Armor

The Shield of Faith

The Roman shield was more than defense. It was survival. Nearly four feet tall, curved to cover the body, built of wood layered with leather and soaked in oil, it quenched fiery arrows. When soldiers formed ranks, they overlapped those shields, creating a wall no flame could break through. With that image in mind, Paul writes, *"Above all, taking the shield of faith, wherewith ye shall be able to quench all the fiery darts of the wicked"* (Ephesians 6:16).

Faith is your living defense against everything the enemy hurls, fear, accusation, doubt, and despair. Faith doesn't deny the fire. It defies its power. Every dart that would pierce the mind or heart is extinguished when it meets the oil-soaked surface of trust in God's Word.

"Thou, O LORD, art a shield for me; my glory, and the lifter up of mine head" (Psalm 3:3). That verse is not poetic exaggeration. It's spiritual fact on the field of battle. When faith rises, fear falls silent.

I remember a season when everything familiar seemed uncertain, a diagnosis that shook a family in our church, rumors that stirred questions, and needs that outgrew our resources. I can still recall standing in the sanctuary after prayer meeting, lights dimmed, wondering how we would make it through another week. Fear whispered through every conversation: *"What if this fails? What if help doesn't come?"* But faith began to speak louder.

We gathered each morning in the fellowship hall, Bibles open, reading Psalm 91 aloud together: *"He shall cover thee with his feathers, and under his wings shalt thou trust"* (Psalm 91:4). The sound was soft at first, trembling, but day by day it grew stronger, like shields locking in place. The circumstances did not vanish, but the fear did. Faith didn't remove the storm. It lifted the shield until peace returned. Not because faith is strong in itself, but because it rests in the strength of Christ (Hebrews 12:2).

**Faith lifted
is fear silenced.**

That is how the shield of faith works. It must be lifted. Faith left lying on the ground, unused, protects no one. You must take it up daily, choosing to believe what God has said rather than what you feel or see. When fiery darts of doubt or accusation come, hold Scripture before emotion and let truth absorb the impact.

The shield is also communal. No soldier stood alone. When the line formed, each man's shield protected the one beside him. That unity was strength, and it still is. This is why the church matters. When one believer grows weary, another's faith covers him until strength returns. A church that stands together in faith becomes a fortress the enemy cannot breach.

"*So then faith cometh by hearing, and hearing by the word of God*" (Romans 10:17). Faith quenches because it connects you to God's power and promises. It draws life from the Word of God and turns those promises into living protection. As you stay in the Word, faith stays soaked, ready for fire, ready for war.

So then, lift the shield. Hold fast to the Word that cannot fail. Cover others when their arms grow tired, and let them cover you. The same God who defends the sparrow will not forsake the soldier.

The flames may fly, but they will die against the faith that stands in Christ.

The Helmet of Salvation

The Roman helmet was built for endurance. Forged of metal and lined with leather, it guarded both the head and the face. When a soldier placed it on, his vision narrowed forward, his hearing sharpened, and his mind settled into readiness. Once the helmet was in place, he was prepared for whatever the enemy brought.

Paul writes, "*And take the helmet of salvation*" (Ephesians 6:17). Salvation protects your mind, the very ground the enemy targets first. Before the enemy conquers a life, he first captures a thought. That is why this piece of armor reaches back to what we studied in Chapter 5, "*The Battleground: Before the Enemy Conquers Your Life, He First Captures Your Thoughts.*" The battle begins in the mind, and salvation secures that field.

Assurance is your mental armor. It protects the mind from lies and

Chapter 7: The Armor

doubt. The believer who knows he is saved thinks differently, prays differently, and faces temptation differently. *"For God hath not appointed us to wrath, but to obtain salvation by our Lord Jesus Christ"* (1 Thessalonians 5:9). That truth steadies perception when everything else feels uncertain.

I think of a man who battled guilt for years. Every mistake replayed in his mind like a broken record. He would say, "Pastor, I know God forgave me, but I can't forgive myself." His eyes carried the weight of old failures, and even in prayer his shoulders stayed tense, as if he expected judgment to fall again.

One afternoon, while reading Romans 8 together, his voice faltered at the words, "There is therefore now no condemnation to them which are in Christ Jesus" (Romans 8:1). He stopped mid-verse, tears rising, and whispered, *"Nothing, not even me."* It was as if a helmet locked into place, sealing off the noise of condemnation. The voices that once accused him grew faint. Peace settled over him, not emotion first, but understanding. His mind finally rested where his salvation already stood: secure in Christ alone.

That is the protection the helmet brings. It guards against mental fatigue and spiritual confusion. The enemy thrives on suggestion: *"Maybe God has forgotten you... perhaps you've gone too far."* But salvation answers, *"...he which hath begun a good work in you will perform it until the day of Jesus Christ"* (Philippians 1:6).

You do not wear the helmet of salvation to earn safety. You wear it because you're already safe in Him, saved by grace through faith, not of works, but by His finished redemption (Ephesians 2:8–9). Assurance doesn't make you careless. It makes you courageous. It frees the mind from self-defense so that faith can stay focused on obedience.

"For he put on righteousness as a breastplate, and an helmet of salvation upon his head" (Isaiah 59:17). That verse shows us that God Himself wears what He gives. The same divine armor that guarded His victory now guards your thoughts.

The mind that rests in salvation will not be ruled by fear.

Spiritual Warfare: Building Your Battle Plan

So then, take up the helmet. Renew your mind each day with the truth that you belong to Christ. When condemnation whispers, remember whose name is written across your armor.

Even in the fiercest conflict, the believer who knows he is saved can think clearly, pray boldly, and rest securely. Once the helmet is on, the battle may reach the ears, but it cannot reach the heart.

A Final Word on The Armor

You've put on every piece now. Truth fastened. Righteousness guarding your heart. Peace steadying your steps. Faith lifted as your shield. Salvation securing your mind.

Weapons win battles, but armor sustains warriors.

The enemy will press. The fight will come. But you are not standing in your own strength. You are standing in the Lord's, covered by armor forged in His victory.

So stand. Not in fear, but in faith. Not holding on to survive, but standing firm to testify that your God reigns.

When the day of battle comes, and it will, you'll be ready. Not because you're perfect, but because He is faithful. Not because the fight is easy, but because the victory is already yours in Christ.

The battle may rage, but the victory belongs to the Lord and to every believer who stands in Him.

7

BUILD YOUR BATTLE PLAN

THE ARMOR

You have learned how to fight, and now you must learn how to defend. Spiritual warfare does not end when the first battle is won. Often, the greater test comes afterward, when the attack lingers, when the enemy fights without retreat, and when there is no sign of relief. This is where many believers become discouraged. Not because they lack weapons, but because they grow weary of the war.

This *battle plan* is not about keeping busy. It is about remaining focused, clothed in the armor of God, settled in Christ's victory, and prepared to endure until the Lord brings resolution.

Purpose of This Battle Plan

The purpose of this battle plan is to train you to defend yourself when the battle does not immediately end.

This plan is designed to help you:
- Stay armored and positioned
- Recognize pressure aimed at reclaiming ground
- Maintain obedience and peace under sustained attack
- Endure without retreating or forcing outcomes

Step 1: Put On the Armor

Armor that is not worn daily will not be ready when the battle comes. The enemy does not announce his advance. He strikes when you are least prepared. If you wait until the arrows are already flying to reach for your shield, you will already be exposed.

This is why you must put on the full armor of God every day. Do it deliberately and consciously. Do it before the day begins, and do it before you enter any season where you know the fight will intensify.

How to Do It?

Scripture is clear about how the armor is put on. After listing each piece, Paul immediately calls the believer to prayer. *"Praying always with all prayer and supplication in the Spirit"* (Ephesians 6:18). The armor is not assumed or activated by intention alone. It is taken up through deliberate prayer before God.

As you come before the Lord, you acknowledge your dependence, place yourself under His authority, and choose to stand in what He has provided rather than your own strength. Prayer is not something added after the armor. It is how the armor is received and worn.

Now It's Your Turn:

Pray through each piece deliberately. Do not rush. Do not assume. Speak these before the Lord as acts of obedience and dependence.

☐ I have fastened ***the belt of truth*** by bringing my thoughts back under God's Word instead of letting emotion, assumption, or distortion run unchecked.

☐ I have put on ***the breastplate of righteousness*** by standing in what Christ has done for me, not defending myself, excusing sin, or trying to prove my worth.

☐ I have ***shod my feet with the preparation of the gospel of peace*** by choosing to walk steadily in the peace Christ secured, refusing to allow fear to dictate my steps.

☐ I have lifted ***the shield of faith*** by choosing to trust what God has said instead of rehearsing worst-case scenarios or feeding doubt.

☐ I have put on ***the helmet of salvation*** by resting in the settled assurance of my salvation and rejecting condemnation, accusation, and doubt.

Reflection

Do not rush past this. Pause and answer honestly before the Lord.

What truth from God's Word do I need to hold tightly today?

Where am I tempted to rely on myself instead of resting in Christ?

Step 2: Hold Your Position

The enemy does not always aim for sudden destruction. More often, he applies steady pressure, waiting for fatigue, frustration, or impatience to cause you to react.

Scripture does not call you to constant fighting, but to endurance. *"That ye may be able to withstand in the evil day, and having done all, to stand"* (Ephesians 6:13).

How to Do It?

When the attack persists, resist the urge to fix, explain, escape, or force an outcome. Standing means remaining obedient and settled in what God has already made clear, even when circumstances do not change.

You do not stand by holding tighter to yourself.
You stand by leaning harder on the Lord.

Standing requires discernment. You must recognize where the attack is trying to move you and refuse to give ground there. Faith is not proven by works, but by remaining steady when doing something feels necessary.

Now It's Your Turn

Slow down. Breathe. Answer honestly before the Lord.

- ☐ I recognize that spiritual attacks do not mean failure or abandonment by God.

- ☐ I refuse to react emotionally or make decisions driven by fear, frustration, or fatigue.

- ☐ I am choosing to remain obedient where God has already spoken.

- ☐ I am trusting God to sustain me rather than trusting myself.

Reflection

What area of my life is under the most attack right now?

What ground am I being tempted to give up?
(peace, faith, obedience, or trust)

If I acted right now, would it be obedience, or would it be escape?

PART FOUR

THE STRATEGY OF VICTORY

Victory is not random, it's the result of order, obedience, and unity under the Spirit's command.

8

THE MINDSET OF A WARRIOR

Learning to think like a soldier of Christ.

You've come a long way in this fight already. You've learned to spot the enemy's attacks, to recognize the pressure when it rises, to hold your ground when everything inside wants to give in. But seeing the battle coming isn't the same as winning it. The Bible tells us to be "...*doers of the word, and not hearers only*..." (James 1:22). You can understand the enemy's strategy, name the lie he's feeding you, and still lose ground if your mind isn't trained for war.

That's where the warrior mindset changes everything. It's the turning point. You stop just surviving—barely making it through the day. You start preparing, standing strong, and advancing with purpose. God didn't save you to scrape by, hoping the next attack won't finish you off. He saved you to overcome, to take back what the enemy stole, and to live in the victory Christ already won.

I've seen this shift in people right in our church. There was a brother who came to me worn out, his mind racing with doubt, fear, and old habits he couldn't shake. He knew the attacks were spiritual. He could name them. But every time they hit, he reacted, chased quick

Spiritual Warfare: Build Your Battle Plan

fixes, and burned out trying harder in his own strength. We sat down, opened the Word, and prayed together. Over time, he stopped reacting and started training his mind. He learned to bring every thought under Christ's command. Today, he's not just holding on. He's helping others do the same. That's the warrior mindset. It turns wounded believers into steady soldiers.

I once knew a woman who loved the Lord with everything in her. You could see it in her worship, hear it in her prayers, and feel it when she served. She genuinely wanted to grow, to walk closer with Jesus. But every time she stepped into a new relationship, the same heartbreaking pattern played out.

It always started the same way. A man would come along who seemed to check the boxes. He talked about God, quoted a verse or two, showed up to a service, and said he supported her faith. At first, it felt like an answer to prayer. She'd convinced herself this one was different.

But slowly, almost without her noticing, things changed. Church started feeling optional. *"We'll go next week,"* he'd say, and she'd agree. Time in the Word dried up because evenings were spent with him. Convictions she once held tight began to bend, just a little here, a little there, until she barely recognized herself. What used to feed her soul now felt like a burden she could set aside for a while.

Then it would end. The relationship would crash and leave her hurt, confused, and empty. She'd come back to the altar weeping, genuinely broken, promising the Lord, *"This time I'll wait. This time I'll do it right."* Her repentance was real. Her desire to change was sincere. I never doubted her heart.

But the cycle kept repeating. Not because she didn't love Jesus enough. Not because her tears weren't honest. It repeated because she was fighting the wrong way. She was relying on willpower, on promises to try harder next time, on emotional resolve after the pain hit. What she needed wasn't another surge of determination. She needed obedience before the feelings ever took over.

She needed to learn to bring her desires, her loneliness, her longings to the Lord and leave them there. To trust His timing instead of grasping for relief. To submit her emotions to His truth instead of letting her emotions lead her into compromise.

Chapter 8: The Mindset of a Warrior

I watched the Lord finally break that cycle in her life, but only after she stopped trusting her own strength and started practicing daily obedience in the quiet places.

Maybe that story sounds familiar. Maybe it is not relationships but something else, an emotion, a habit, a temptation, or a weakness that keeps pulling you off course. You start strong. You feel determined. You tell yourself this time will be different. But then the emotion fades, the pressure rises, and the cycle repeats. That is what happens when we depend on determination instead of surrender.

God never called us to overcome in our own strength. He called us to obey. And until obedience becomes the foundation rather than emotion, we will keep losing the same battles again and again. For our strength is made perfect only through His grace (2 Corinthians 12:9).

The warrior's mindset isn't about fighting harder. It's about trusting God enough to wait.

God is shaping your mind for battle. He's teaching you to bring *"...every thought to the obedience of Christ"* (2 Corinthians 10:5). This is not gentle advice but the language of warfare. Thoughts are examined, tested against truth, and brought under Christ's authority rather than allowed to run free.

The strongest warriors in God's army aren't the ones who shout the loudest or move the fastest. They're the most focused. Victory isn't won out on the open field when the battle finally breaks loose. It starts long before that, right in your mind.

Distraction kills quicker than any weapon the enemy can throw at you. An unguarded mind is nothing less than an open door, inviting the devil to walk right in and set up camp.

Your body has armor, yes. God gave you that protection. But your mind has something far more powerful: the Spirit working through the Word, *"the sword of the Spirit, which is the word of God"* (Ephesians 6:17), the truth that sanctifies you (John 17:17). That's your offensive weapon. That's what cuts through lies and strongholds.

God isn't raising up emotional sprinters who light up the room for a moment and then crash when the feelings fade. He's building steady men and women who endure, who learn to hear His voice clear above

Spiritual Warfare: Build Your Battle Plan

the noise, who grip His promises tight, and who keep obeying even when the pressure squeezes so hard you can barely breathe.

This mindset doesn't grow in the spotlight. It grows in prayer when no one else is watching. It grows in the Word when it's just you and God in the room. Jesus said, *"But thou, when thou prayest, enter into thy closet, and when thou hast shut thy door, pray to thy Father which is in secret; and thy Father which seeth in secret shall reward thee openly"* (Matthew 6:6). Those hidden hours are what make the difference. They turn weary survivors into warriors who stand unshaken when the storm finally hits.

God isn't just trying to help you panic less today. He's preparing you to push forward tomorrow. Survival might get you through the next attack. But discipline, day after day obedience in the secret place, gets you through the whole war.

Transformation opens your eyes.
Training keeps you standing.

Patience: The Strategy That Holds

What happens when the fight doesn't end quickly like you hoped? When it's not one attack you can shake off, but a long, continuous battle that just keeps coming? When your prayers start feeling like whispers into an empty room, and that heavy weight you've begged God to lift is still sitting square on your shoulders, day after day?

That's where Patience shows up. Not in the first rush of faith when everything feels possible. It shows itself in the long stretch afterward, when feelings fade, when the excitement is gone, and all that's left is obedience.

You need Patience to inherit the promises. The Bible says, *"For ye have need of patience, that, after ye have done the will of God, ye might receive the promise"* (Hebrews 10:36). This isn't about gritting your teeth or forcing yourself to hang on a little longer in your own strength. It's staying faithful when it's hard, trusting when nothing on the outside looks any different.

No one is born with patience. God builds it in you. He starts with grace that softens and changes your heart. Then He trains you, day by

Chapter 8: The Mindset of a Warrior

day, reshaping your habits so you learn to stay steady when the fire gets hot.

I think of a sister at church who lived this out. She was the only believer in her office, and her boss threatened the staff that he didn't want any *"religious talk."* Colleagues mocked her when she bowed her head to pray over lunch or when she refused to join the gossip. The attack came constantly. First it began with little digs, unfair assignments, and then whispers behind her back. Every day felt like a spiritual attack. She could have quit, found an easier job, or just kept quiet to fit in. Most people would have understood.

But she stayed. She obeyed God in the small things by saying kind words even when she was hurt, doing honest work even when it went unnoticed, and by being a quiet witness even when it cost her. She endured the hostility, trusting God's timing. And over time, that patience didn't just keep her standing. It opened doors the enemy never expected. One coworker started watching her steadiness and asked questions. Then another. Eventually, God used her faithfulness to lead three of them to the Lord.

Her patience wasn't loud or dramatic. It was quiet, faithful, day after day. And it bore fruit that hell never saw coming.

Soldiers don't show up to war ready. They train, long and hard. Faith grows the same way, *"from faith to faith"* (Romans 1:17). One obedience today, another tomorrow. No crowds cheering, no applause. Just quiet choices that build the *spiritual muscle* for the bigger fights ahead.

God trains you to prepare you, not to punish you. Every small, hidden obedience is rehearsal for the storm. *"So then faith cometh by hearing, and hearing by the word of God"* (Romans 10:17).

Emotion can light the fire, but it always fades. Patience is what holds when our *"feelings"* go quiet. That's why God uses these long seasons to mature us. We inherit the promises through *"faith and patience"* (Hebrews 6:12), not through hype or emotional highs.

The Spirit doesn't always remove the weight right when we ask. Sometimes He strengthens us to carry it. *"My grace is sufficient for thee: for my strength is made perfect in weakness"* (2 Corinthians 12:9). In that place, conviction turns into stability. Fragile belief grows into real patience. Shaky faith becomes unshakeable.

Spiritual Warfare: Build Your Battle Plan

You prove your faith not when you feel strong, but when you're empty, worn down, and still obey the Lord anyway. That's patience: obedience stretched over time.

Patience is not trying harder.
It's trusting deeper.

What Patience Builds in You

Let me tell you what patience, real biblical patience, does inside a believer. Nothing else can touch it. Nothing else can produce it.

Patience brings a peace that holds steady even when everything around you is shaking, falling apart, coming undone. That's the *"...peace of God, which passeth all understanding..."* that guards your heart and your mind through Christ Jesus (Philippians 4:7). Peace isn't the absence of trouble. It's the deep, settled assurance that God is right there with you in the middle of it.

It gives you clarity too. When emotions are screaming loud, trying to drown out truth, patience keeps your mind anchored so you can think biblically. A heart renewed by the Word begins to see God's truth over the enemy's lies, and God's way over the pull of the flesh. And it builds real strength, a spiritual backbone that refuses to bend no matter how hard the attack hits.

You end up lacking nothing because your dependence is fully on Him alone. The Bible says it plain: *"...let patience have her perfect work, that ye may be perfect and entire, wanting nothing"* (James 1:4).

I've counseled so many folks who started out shaky, tossed around by every wave that came crashing in. Doubt one day, fear the next, discouragement pulling them under. But as they endured, as they kept obeying God through the long hard grind, when nothing seemed to change, something beautiful happened. They turned into rocks. Not actual rocks, of course, but they became unmovable, steadfast, and ready for whatever came next.

That's the enemy's nightmare: a child of God who stands firm not because the fight is easy, but because the Lord has trained them, through the long seasons to endure.

Chapter 8: The Mindset of a Warrior

That's the mark of a mature warrior. Someone who has learned not just to fight hard, but to be patient and to stand firm.

**Let patience
have her perfect work.**

God's Purpose in Your Trials

God never wastes a trial. Not one. He doesn't allow the spiritual attack just to break you down or wear you out. He uses it to build you up, to shape you into someone mature, steady, and complete.

Every delay that frustrates you. Every unanswered prayer that keeps you up at night. Every long, dark season that feels endless. It all has purpose in His hands. Nothing is random with God. Nothing is pointless. He's forming believers who lack nothing because their trust is rooted in Him alone. Patience does that work: it quiets the emotional roller coaster, steadies your mind when thoughts spin wild, and roots your heart deep where storms can't uproot you.

Look at Job. In one day, he lost his wealth, his servants, and his ten children. Then Satan struck his body with boils from head to foot. He sat in ashes, scraping his sores, questions pouring out of a broken heart. Everything that could go wrong did. Yet through it all, he held on and declared, *"Though he slay me, yet will I trust in him"* (Job 13:15). His patience looked like standing still, trusting God when absolutely nothing made sense.

Then look at Paul. Beaten with rods, whipped, stoned, shipwrecked, imprisoned, and rejected at every turn. Yet he kept moving forward. He wrote, *"I press toward the mark for the prize of the high calling of God in Christ Jesus"* (Philippians 3:14). His patience looked like obedience in motion, one painful, faithful step after another.

Two men. Two completely different battles. One powerful truth: patience is nothing less than obedience stretched over time. Two men.

**God uses trials not to test your limits,
but to perfect your faith.**

Spiritual Warfare: Build Your Battle Plan

Who You Were vs. Who You're Becoming

This is where the rubber meets the road. Before patience takes root in your life, you're easily knocked off course. The attack comes, and it rattles you hard. Delays frustrate you to the point of anger. Disappointment hits, and it sends you reeling. Your faith rides the wave of feelings: high and on fire one day, low and questioning everything the next.

That was a lot of us before the Lord started doing His deeper work.

But as patience builds in you, something real changes. You become steady. You get *"rooted and built up in him, and stablished in the faith"* (Colossians 2:7). No more getting tossed around by every wind that blows. You stand firm because your confidence is in God, not in your circumstances.

**It's a total shift.
Night and day.**

Let's be honest with each other. Patience grows where the fight is the fiercest, right in your mind where Satan works overtime to build his strongholds, brick by lying brick, until you feel trapped in the same old cycles you can't break.

I've seen it in believers who truly love God with all their heart. They fall into the same patterns over and over. Drugs. Porn. Bad relationships. Late-night regrets that crush them the next morning. Sunday they're in church lifting their hands in worship, weeping at the altar, promising the Lord, *"This time it's going to be different."* And I believe their repentance is genuine every single time.

But come Thursday, they're right back in the mess. Not because they're faking their love for Jesus. They're just fighting the wrong way.

They fight like sinners, trying harder, promising bigger, and hoping next time they'll feel stronger.

A soldier fights differently.

He trains daily.

Chapter 8: The Mindset of a Warrior

He obeys orders even when he doesn't feel like it.
He holds his ground no matter what.
The sinner says, *"I'll try again when I feel stronger."*
The soldier says, *"I'll obey even when I feel weak."*

Emotion can't defeat a spiritual enemy. Tears don't tear down strongholds. Good intentions and desire alone don't bring lasting victory.

Until the mind is trained, until obedience becomes stronger than impulse, the attacks keep winning.

But listen with hope, because this is the gospel truth for you. You weren't saved to barely survive. You were saved to stand. Christ didn't redeem you so you could crawl through life wounded and defeated. He called you to rise as a warrior: steady, trained, unshakeable.

The enemy fears enduring believers because they don't retreat. Patience breaks his grip. Temptation loses its power when your mind refuses to yield to it.

You're not fighting for victory like it's still up for grabs. You're fighting from victory, because Christ already won it. Satan wants you to believe you're weak, trapped, and forever defined by your past. That's a lie. You are Christ's soldier, filled with His Spirit.

The war is real. But so is the power living in you.

Let patience finish its work. Keep obeying today, even when you feel weak. Stay rooted in Him.

**Patience turns broken believers
into unbreakable warriors.**

Thinking Under Command

Every good soldier knows you don't fight the battle on your own terms. The battlefield is no place for independent thoughts or ideas. If you break formation and follow your own decisions instead of the commander's instructions, you don't just put yourself in danger. You endanger others.

The same holds true in spiritual warfare. The mind of a warrior is a mind under God's authority. Every thought must be captured, every idea examined, and every decision submitted to the Commander's voice. This isn't about suppressing thoughts or pretending questions don't exist. It's the discipline of training your mind to respond to God's Word rather than your emotions or the enemy's lies.

An undisciplined mind is like an unguarded gate. One breach, and the enemy floods the fortress. That's why Paul wrote about *"...bringing into captivity every thought to the obedience of Christ"* (2 Corinthians 10:5). It's warfare language on purpose. First, you capture those rogue thoughts, chain them, and test them against the truth of God's Word. And then you force them to bow to Christ.

I've counseled believers who were sharp, knew the Word, loved the Lord, but their minds were still running wild. Doubt would strike, and they'd spiral fast. Fear would whisper, and they'd react before they even thought to pray. They weren't weak in faith. Their minds simply hadn't been trained to submit yet.

Once they started practicing this discipline, pausing when the thought came, praying right then, and running it straight through Scripture—everything began to change. Calm returned in the middle of chaos. Steadiness showed up when the storm was at its worst. They stayed anchored to the Commander's voice, unmoved by the enemy's threats.

Obedience becomes your weapon.
Discipline becomes your shield.

Formation Thinking: Shields Locked

A warrior doesn't last long fighting solo. The fiercest soldiers in history knew this truth deep in their bones. Your strength multiplies when minds and movements align. Look at the Roman legions. They didn't win empires with lone heroes charging ahead, swinging wildly. Each man's shield was made to cover himself and the soldier beside him.

In their testudo formation, they locked shields tight. Front row solid. Sides angled. Top like a roof. Arrows rained down and bounced off harmlessly. The enemy could scream, charge, throw everything they had, but that shell held. Alone, any one of them would have fallen quick. Together, they were a moving fortress no army could easily break. That's formation thinking.

Chapter 8: The Mindset of a Warrior

You were never meant to fight this spiritual war alone. When you're isolated, cut off, handling it all by yourself, you become the enemy's favorite target. Satan doesn't always need a dramatic kill shot. He just pulls you away from fellowship, from accountability, from real community. Then he wears you down slowly, until you collapse under the weight of your own thoughts, your own struggles, your own secrets.

But when you lock shields with other believers, when obedience binds your hearts together, when worship lifts your voices as one, when prayer covers each other's weaknesses, something powerful happens. The enemy starts losing ground that he thought he owned. Unity becomes your armor. Accountability becomes your cover. Fellowship becomes your strength.

I've seen it in our church with a young man who came in broken, addicted, and ashamed. He tried fighting alone for years, white-knuckling, hiding, promising God he'd do better. But when he finally got planted in a church, opened up in a small group, let brothers lock shields with him through prayer and truth, something changed for him. The enemy couldn't penetrate that formation. He's free today, and now he's the one helping others stand.

The devil fears a church moving in formation because he can't penetrate a wall of believers standing shoulder to shoulder under Christ.

Unity isn't about everybody liking the same music or having the same personality. It's about every single one of us submitting to the same Commander.

In Rome, ego or drift could get the whole unit killed. The same is true in Christ's body. Distraction, pride, offense, those things break the line faster than any sword. A divided army stalls out and gets picked apart. A united body advances and takes ground.

My shield guards you. Yours guards me.
We stand or fall together.
That's formation thinking!

Spiritual Warfare: Build Your Battle Plan

The Focused Mind and The Finished Race

Formation holds your line strong, but focus is what advances it. You can be perfectly aligned with other believers, shields locked tight, discipline sharp as it's ever been, but if your attention drifts even a little, the whole line can collapse at the first unexpected hit. The soldier who survives and finishes the race isn't the one trying to watch everything happening around him. He's the one whose eyes stay fixed straight ahead on the Commander.

The enemy's greatest weapon isn't always overwhelming force. More often it's distraction. He pulls your eyes off course with pressure, busyness, fear, temptation, comparison, anything he can throw to get you looking sideways instead of forward.

When you're distracted, you start losing ground long before the fight even looks lost. Scripture commands us clear and direct: *"Looking unto Jesus the author and finisher of our faith"* (Hebrews 12:2).

Focus isn't pretending trouble doesn't exist. It's seeing right through the trouble to God's work on the other side.

Paul lived this out while chained and beaten in prison. He wrote, *"I press toward the mark for the prize of the high calling of God in Christ Jesus"* (Philippians 3:14). Circumstances screamed loud around him: pain, rejection, uncertainty, darkness closing in. But his faith was louder. He kept his eyes locked on the prize.

The focused mind measures progress by obedience, not by results. It moves forward relentlessly, one faithful step at a time, no matter how loud the circumstances get. When your mind is fixed on Christ, discouragement can't hold you, fear loses its authority, and distraction loses its power.

So where are your eyes today? What's pulling them sideways? Is it worry, comparison, busyness, or pain? The race isn't over. The prize is still ahead. Turn your eyes back to Jesus, the author and finisher of your faith. Lock your focus on Him.

Keep looking forward.
Keep pressing on.

Chapter 8: The Mindset of a Warrior

The Calm Before the Attack

Every army knows the hush right before the charge. The shouting stops. The dust settles. Weapons are ready. Silence hangs heavy with what's coming.

Soldiers check their armor one last time. They tighten their grip on their shields. They lean forward into the line. It's not fear holding them there. It's readiness. They remember why they fight, who leads them, and what's at stake.

God brings us to those same moments spiritually. The calm before the attack is where He calls us to examine the battlefield before we advance against the enemy. He doesn't bring the silence to condemn us. He brings it to prepare us, to strengthen our conviction, to restore our clarity, to fortify our resolve.

A soldier takes inventory before charging into the battle. He checks his wounds, loyalty, readiness, and his heart.

So what war is happening inside you right now? What stronghold have you allowed to stand too long? What distraction is stealing your focus? What sin have you promised to conquer *"eventually"* instead of surrendering today?

A soldier who ignores his wounds bleeds out on the field. One who pretends he's fine collapses when the line advances. This moment of quiet is for you to kneel. Pray with David, *"Search me, O God, and know my heart: try me, and know my thoughts: and see if there be any wicked way in me, and lead me in the way everlasting"* (Psalm 139:23–24).

The enemy hates this calm. The devil trembles when you grow quiet before God. Silence is where the Spirit speaks, where conviction replaces confusion, clarity replaces panic, and faithful obedience replaces fearful emotions.

This is the calm before the attack.

If the Spirit is stirring or convicting your heart right now, don't resist Him. Don't push it off. Lay it down. Confess it. Repent of it. Surrender it fully. Let Him prepare you.

The warrior who kneels before God will stand before any enemy.

Spiritual Warfare: Build Your Battle Plan

The Rallying Charge

Then the quiet breaks, and the silence ends. The Commander's voice rings clear through the stillness.

The waiting has done its work. The kneeling warrior rises, not trembling, not unsure, but resolved. He stands not on fleeting feelings, but on rock-solid submission. His strength flows from obedience, not from adrenaline. The calm has prepared him. Now the orders come.

The call to advance doesn't wait for your life to feel comfortable or circumstances to soften. God commands movement when surrender has shaped your trust, when your heart is ready to follow without hesitation. Hear the directive: *"Finally, my brethren, be strong in the Lord, and in the power of his might. Put on the whole armour of God"* (Ephesians 6:10–11).

These words aren't gentle encouragement.

They're a military directive from your heavenly Commander.

This isn't the time for you to retreat.
This isn't the moment for you to negotiate with sin.
This isn't the hour to wait until obedience feels convenient.

This is the hour to rise.
This is the hour to fight.
This is the hour to advance.

Lift your shield with confidence.
Plant your feet on the ground God gave you.
Grip the sword of the Spirit firmly.
Fix your eyes on Christ, and don't look back.
The enemy has stolen your peace, your worship, your resolve.
Reclaim it through discipline, patience, and obedience.

The warrior who kneels before God will stand before any enemy.

Go. Hear the command loud and clear: *"Submit yourselves therefore to God. Resist the devil, and he will flee from you"* (James 4:7).

Chapter 8: The Mindset of a Warrior

Reclaim the ground the enemy stole from you. Break those old patterns that once broke you. Stand firm where you once fell. Fight bold where you once surrendered. Advance strong where you once retreated.

You're a soldier in the living God's army. Trained by His grace. Strengthened by endurance. Covered by Christ's precious blood. Empowered by the Holy Spirit who lives within you.

The enemy may roar loud, but Christ has already won the victory. You're not fighting for it anymore. You're fighting from it.

So hear the rallying cry today.
The Commander is calling you forward.

Resist.
Reclaim.
Advance.

In the power of His might.
In the authority of His name.
In the certainty of His victory.

Forward, soldier!
The King is with you.
The battle belongs to Him.

8

BUILD YOUR BATTLE PLAN

THE MINDSET

You know that feeling when the attack comes out of nowhere, and before you can even pray or quote a verse, your mind has already gone blank. First fear sets in, followed by doubt, and then all the old lies you thought you had dealt with come rushing into your mind. You fight back, you stand for a moment, but the damage is already done because your thoughts beat you to the punch.

Most spiritual battles aren't lost in the big, obvious moment of temptation or trial. They are lost when your mind reaches for the wrong thoughts first. You win the victory by training your mind long before the attacks ever start.

Purpose of This Battle Plan

The purpose of this battle plan is to train your mind to think on truth when the battle does not immediately end.

This plan is designed to help you:

- Identify thoughts that weaken your spiritual resistance.
- Replace those thoughts with disciplined, biblical resolve.
- Anchor your identity in God's truth rather than emotions.
- Establish a mindset that is already prepared before the next battle begins.

Step 1: Identify Thought Patterns

Every one of us thinks in patterns. Some of those patterns build up your faith and help you stand. Others quietly chip away at it, making you more vulnerable than you realize.

The enemy rarely attacks with something new. He just keeps coming back to the same sore spots, the same pressure points, hoping your mind will default to the old way of thinking instead of resisting with truth.

Action:

Think back over recent battles, times of attack, discouragement, temptation, or conflict. Answer honestly.

When a spiritual attack begins, my first instinct is to think about:

☐ My fear:
"This feels overwhelming or out of control."

☐ My failure:
"I messed up again."

☐ My feelings:
"I feel anxious, discouraged, angry, or numb."

☐ My past:
"I've been here before, and it never ends well."

☐ My circumstances:
"If things around me would change, this would stop."

☐ God's truth:
"What does God say, and what has He already promised?"

Write your most common first thoughts here:

Step 2: Expose the Lie

Behind every unhealthy thought pattern is a lie that has been allowed to live in your mind, unchallenged, repeated, or simply tolerated.

The enemy doesn't have to overwhelm you with power. He just needs you to believe something that isn't true. One lie, left in place, is enough to weaken you, steal your peace, and open the door to defeat.

Action:

Look back at the patterns you identified in **Step 1**. Be honest and specific as you complete these.

"When I am under attack, I often believe the lie that..."

What does God's Word say that directly contradicts this lie?
(You do not need to write the verse yet — just the truth.)

Step 3: Establish Your Warrior Identity

You will always fight inconsistently if you are unclear about who you are. A warrior mindset isn't built on confidence in yourself. It's built on crystal-clear identity in Christ, the unshakable truth of who He says you are.

Action:

Complete each sentence deliberately.

"Because I belong to Christ, I am not fighting for victory, I am fighting from _____." Romans 8:37

"When the enemy attacks my mind, I must remember that God has given me _____, not fear." 2 Timothy 1:7

Write one sentence that defines who you are in this war:

"In Christ, I am _____."

Step 4: Choose Your Thoughts

If you do not choose the right thought intentionally, the enemy will choose it for you. He'll push the old lie, the familiar fear, the one that has knocked you down before. But you can decide right now what your mind will run to instead.

Action:

Pray and ask the Lord to show you the truth your mind needs most right now. Then select one. Keep it short. One sentence you can say when everything feels chaotic.

This truth must be:
- Biblical
- Simple
- Repeatable under pressure

Write it as a clear statement, not a paragraph.

"When the battle begins, I will return to this truth: _____
_____."

"When the battle begins, I will return to this truth: _____
_____."

"When the battle begins, I will return to this truth: _____
_____."

Examples:
"When the battle begins, I will return to this truth:
- "God is with me and will never leave me."
- "I am more than a conqueror through Christ who loves me."
- "The Lord is my shepherd; I shall not want."

Step 5: Commit to Mental Discipline

A warrior does not let his mind wander freely in the middle of a fight. He guards it, directs it, and brings it back to truth every time it starts to drift.

Action:

Write one deliberate commitment you will practice this week.

"This week, when my thoughts begin to drift toward _____,

I will intentionally respond by _____*."*

"This week, when my thoughts begin to drift toward _____,

I will intentionally respond by _____*."*

(Examples: *prayer, Scripture, redirecting the thought, speaking truth aloud.*)

9

THE MOVEMENT OF THE SPIRIT

Learning to operate under the Commander's direction.

You know those times when obedience looks like doing something big. You can point to it clear as day. You changed that habit that had you bound for years. You started that ministry or small group. You fixed what was broken in your home. You pushed through when every voice said quit. And it feels good, doesn't it? You can see progress. You know you're walking with God because your hands are busy and your days are full of purpose.

But here's what a lot of us miss. God doesn't always measure obedience by how much we're getting done.

He looks deeper. He sees the heart. The Bible says, *"For the LORD seeth not as man seeth; for man looketh on the outward appearance, but the LORD looketh on the heart"* (1 Samuel 16:7). Sometimes the most obedient thing you can do is nothing at all. Not laziness. Not giving up. Just standing still, because that's exactly what He told you to do.

I've been there myself. I've worn myself out trying to help God move things along. I've prayed harder, worked longer, and tried to push doors open that were meant to be closed, all because waiting felt wrong. It felt like I wasn't trusting God enough. Like if I just did a little more, spoke up one more time, or tried one more thing, He'd finally bless it and open the door. But that's not how the Spirit leads.

There are seasons in our lives where the next step isn't to move forward. During those times, God calls us to stay, to wait, and to hold our position even when everything inside us is screaming to move. For most people, waiting or being stationary doesn't feel like faithfulness. It feels like failure. We're so used to measuring obedience by *"doing something"* that being still starts to feel irresponsible.

That is exactly when the enemy loves to attack. He knows if he can get you moving before God says go, you'll burn out trying to finish in your own strength what only the Spirit can do. The Bible warns that what God starts in the Spirit can't be finished in the flesh (Galatians 3:3).

That's why James tells us, *"Submit yourselves therefore to God. Resist the devil, and he will flee from you"* (James 4:7). Submission comes first. Resisting the devil often looks like refusing to run ahead.

Waiting on God isn't weakness. It's warfare.

When you find yourself in a season of stillness, don't mistake it for stagnation. God is teaching you to trust His heart when you can't see His hand. He's building patience that busyness alone could never produce.

When Busyness Feels Like Obedience

Most of us don't learn the difference between busyness and truly obeying until we're right in the middle of a spiritual attack. When things are calm, it's easy to wait on the Lord. We can quote the verses, nod along in church, and feel patient. But when the attack hits hard, when the need feels urgent, or when God's silence stretches longer than we can stand, that's when the flesh kicks in.

The flesh doesn't ask, *"What did God say?"*

Chapter 9: The Movement of The Spirit

It asks, *"What can I do right now to fix this?"*

I've watched it happen in good, sincere people. There was a brother in our church who suddenly lost his job. Bills started piling up fast, and he started to feel as though he would never recover from all the debt. He prayed, he believed God for provision, and he trusted the promises. But weeks turned into months with no promise of a job in sight. The pressure continued to grow. So he started applying everywhere, taking interviews that didn't sit right in his spirit, even considering offers that would pull him away from church and ministry. He told himself, *"At least I'm doing something. At least I'm being responsible."* He wasn't lazy. He was desperate.

He moved before God moved.

Every step took him further from peace.

Busyness started feeling like faith. He told himself he was being responsible. But busyness isn't obedience. Doing more isn't trusting more. And when God has said *"be still and wait,"* doing more is actually doing less—less of what He asked.

Scripture states, *"...to obey is better than sacrifice..."* (1 Samuel 15:22). Sincerity doesn't cover disobedience. Good intentions don't cancel stepping out of line.

That's one of the enemy's favorite traps. He doesn't always tempt you to quit serving God altogether. Sometimes he tempts you to rush ahead, do more, and grow weary. He knows a premature move will wear you out faster than standing still ever could.

Busyness is not
the same as obedience.

I remember counseling a young wife whose marriage was falling apart. She loved the Lord. She wanted her home healed more than anything else. So, she read every marriage book she could find, scheduling counseling sessions back-to-back, serving more hours at church, praying harder, fasting longer, and even trying every strategy people suggested. She thought, *"Doing something felt better than doing nothing."*

But every time she tried to get ahead of God's timing, the tension grew worse. The arguments grew hotter, and her peace quickly slipped

Spiritual Warfare: Building Your Battle Plan

further away. She came to me exhausted and said, *"Pastor, I don't know what else to do. I've tried everything."*

In that moment, the Lord showed her the answer wasn't doing more. It was to be still. It was trusting Him enough to stop trying to fix things in her own strength and start waiting on His perfect timing.

That's hard for us, isn't it? Waiting feels risky. It feels like letting go when everything is already slipping through our fingers. But waiting is exactly where real faith grows. That's where the Spirit has room to work without our interference.

Amy as a Diagnostic Mirror

Please allow me to introduce you to Amy. Amy is not a reckless person. She's not unstable. She does not dodge responsibility. Amy loves the Lord deeply, serves faithfully in our church, and lives with real intention. Her life has a steady rhythm of obedience that's been shaped over years, not just a few weeks. She plans carefully, follows through consistently, and finds genuine peace in knowing she's being useful for the kingdom. When she moves, things get done. When she stays busy serving, she feels grounded, like she's right in the center of God's will.

That's exactly why the call to be still unsettled her so much.

When the Spirit placed Amy in a season where waiting was the only clear instruction, it didn't feel like strength. It felt like uncertainty. It felt like isolation. Nothing dramatic had gone wrong. There was no sin to repent of, no sudden crisis demanding an immediate response. The pressure came from somewhere quieter. She was simply held in place without a clear explanation. The ministry she expected to serve in was never assigned. The next opportunity to serve passed her by, too.

At first, she told herself it was temporary. She kept praying, kept serving where she could, kept looking for the door to swing open. But time stretched on, and the silence from heaven remained. The discomfort grew, not because she doubted God's goodness or love, but because she didn't know how to measure faithfulness without doing something. Amy was used to obedience that looked productive, the

Chapter 9: The Movement of The Spirit

kind of obedience you could see or even point to. However, this waiting felt like failure.

The longer it lasted, the more confusing it became. She started asking the same questions so many of us ask in those seasons: *"Did I miss something? Is God waiting on me to do more? Shouldn't I be stepping out, trying harder, or making something happen?"* But deep down, she knew the Lord hadn't given her another step. He had asked her to stand still. And that didn't feel like obedience. It felt like weakness.

I sat with Amy during that season. She'd come in, eyes tired but determined, and say, *"Pastor, I just feel stuck. I want to obey, I want to do something, serve somewhere, but I don't know what He wants me to do."* We opened the Word together, looked at places like Psalm 46:10, *"Be still, and know that I am God"*, and Exodus 14:14, *"The LORD shall fight for you, and ye shall hold your peace"*. The truth was clear, but living it felt foreign. She'd spent years equating fruitfulness with activity. Now God was teaching her that fruitfulness sometimes grows in the soil of stillness.

Over time, as she leaned into that hard obedience of waiting, something beautiful happened. Her peace returned, and it was now deeper than before. When the next step finally came, she walked into it rested, steady, and full of faith instead of frantic energy.

Stillness can feel like failure when you're used to measuring obedience by busyness.

If Amy's story sounds familiar, if you're in a season right now where waiting is the only clear word you have from God, and it's driving you crazy because you're a doer, a fixer, or a mover, don't fight the stillness. Embrace it (Isaiah 40:31).

Battlefield Discipline Under Pressure

Spiritual attacks have a way of exposing exactly how we think about progress. The Bible tells us trials are meant to test and refine our faith (1 Peter 1:6–7). When the attack ramps up, most believers don't drift into laziness. They push harder, do more, and even move faster. That

Spiritual Warfare: Building Your Battle Plan

instinct might work when the ground is steady, and everything seems clear. But when the ground is shaking, doing something without direction becomes a real liability. It's like a soldier sprinting into enemy territory without orders. It looks brave, but it's not smart.

In battle, moving forward without direction only wears you down. It's like a truck stuck deep in the mud. The engine roars loudly, and the wheels spin fast, sending mud flying everywhere, but you're going nowhere. And eventually, you burn out the motor.

That's what happens to so many believers under prolonged attack. They're not undisciplined. They're exhausted. Not because they aren't trying hard enough, but because they've been trying in the wrong direction. They're pushing when the Spirit has said wait. They're acting when the clear order was to stand still.

God's Word reminds us, *"The steps of a good man are ordered by the LORD: and he delighteth in his way"* (Psalm 37:23). And where there is no order, there should be no movement.

The Subtle Danger of Trying to Help God

Some of the sneakiest lies the enemy slips into spiritual warfare sound almost righteous. *"If I care enough, I should act right now." "If I love enough, I should try to fix it myself." "If I really trust God, I should see results soon."*

Caring doesn't give you permission to move without God-given direction. Love doesn't override the Lord's perfect timing. Trust doesn't mean He operates on your schedule.

I've seen good believers jump into hard conversations that weren't Spirit-led at all. I've watched others make big decisions without waiting on a clear word from God. All because the need felt urgent and staying silent felt wrong. Their hearts were sincere. They weren't rebelling. They were just trying to help God out.

Remember Uzzah? The ark of God was on the cart, the oxen stumbled, and the ark started to tip. Uzzah reached out his hand to steady it. Good intention. Natural reaction. You or I would have done the same thing. But God struck him down that day (2 Samuel 6:6–7). Why? Because even right motives don't override God's clear commands. The ark was never to be touched. Period!

Chapter 9: The Movement of The Spirit

If we are not careful, we will do the same thing. Like Uzzah, we might see something shaking and reach out to steady it before asking if God told us to touch it. That's the danger of assuming that a natural burden means we should do it. We think the pressure means it's time for us to move.

But a burden is not the same as permission.

God gives the burden so we'll pray. He gives the command, so we'll move. Until the command comes, the burden is meant to drive us to our knees, not to our feet.

That's where so many of us get into trouble. We feel the weight, so we act. We see the need, so we step in. Even if God hasn't said go. We're stepping out of position. And out of position in battle means exposed, no matter how noble the reason.

If the enemy is pressing you hard and whispering, *"Do something now,"* pause long enough to ask, *"Lord, is this burden Your call to prayer, or Your permission to move?"*

How The Spirit Actually Leads

So how do you know when it's truly the Spirit leading you to wait, or when it's just fear holding you back?

The Bible gives us a clear answer. God doesn't lead through confusion. *"For God is not the author of confusion, but of peace..."* (1 Corinthians 14:33). His voice brings clarity, not chaos. It brings settled peace, even when circumstances remain hard.

How do you keep following God faithfully when nothing seems to be moving? That's not doubting God. That's wanting to get it right. And I understand the struggle, because I've been there, and I've walked with plenty of folks in our church through the same questions.

The Spirit never bypasses what God has already said in His written Word. He illuminates it. He applies it right to your situation. Jesus promised, *"Howbeit when he, the Spirit of truth, is come, he will guide you into all truth"* (John 16:13). That truth is already there in Scripture. The Spirit takes it off the page and makes it alive in your

Spiritual Warfare: Building Your Battle Plan

heart.

So if you're feeling frantic, driven, restless, pushed to move right now or else, that's not the Spirit. That's pressure. The Spirit leads with steady conviction, not emotional urgency that makes you panic.

Here's how to test what you're sensing.

- Does it line up perfectly with Scripture, or is it asking you to step around what the Word clearly says?

- Does the urge grow stronger and clearer when you wait on God in prayer, or does it start to fade and feel fleshly when you slow down and seek Him?

- Is it drawing you closer to Jesus Himself, or is it mostly offering quick relief from the discomfort?

The Spirit uses two main tools to lead you: the *Word* and *conviction*.

The *Word* marks the clear boundaries, the principles that never change. Conviction is how the Spirit applies that truth precisely to where you stand right now.

Conviction isn't loud or rushed. It's firm. It's patient. It stays with you until you respond. It doesn't panic if you take time to pray it through and seek confirmation.

So if you're lacking wisdom about whether to wait or move, ask. The Bible invites you to: *"If any of you lack wisdom, let him ask of God, that giveth to all men liberally, and upbraideth not; and it shall be given him"* (James 1:5). God doesn't hide His will to play games with you. He wants you to know it.

And sometimes the answer is wait.
Not forever. Just for now.

If what you're feeling is restless, frantic, or demanding immediate action, step back. Get into the Word. Get quiet before God. Ask Him to settle your heart with His peace.

Chapter 9: The Movement of The Spirit

Learning The Discipline of Restraint

In our fast-paced world, waiting looks like weakness. Standing still feels like doing nothing. Busyness gets praised. Action gets results. But in God's kingdom, restraint is real strength. The psalmist declared, *"Wait on the LORD: be of good courage, and he shall strengthen thine heart: wait, I say, on the LORD"* (Psalm 27:14). Waiting takes courage. It's not passive. It's an active choice to trust.

Why does God lead us into seasons of stillness? Because some of the deepest lessons only come when everything else stops. Trust grows stronger. Dependence on Him deepens. Patience is built through resistance, the same way muscles are built. You learn in the quiet that God's timing is always perfect, even when it doesn't look productive to anyone watching.

Think about Israel at the Red Sea. Pharaoh's army thundering behind them. Impassable water in front. Every natural instinct screamed panic, run, fight, do something. But God gave the strangest command: *"Fear ye not, stand still, and see the salvation of the LORD which he will shew to you to day"* (Exodus 14:13). Deliverance didn't come from frantic running or clever strategy. It came from obeying in stillness.

If you're in a season where no doors are opening, where the next step isn't clear, don't assume something's wrong. Don't rush to force it open. God may be teaching you restraint, training you to trust His timing instead of your own.

Waiting isn't wasted time.
It's preparation.

James tells us the trying of our faith works patience, and patience finishes its work so we lack nothing (James 1:3–4). That's God's design, not a detour. Stillness isn't punishment. It's development. He's shaping you into someone mature, steady, complete.

So if you're in a season right now where no doors are opening, where the next step isn't clear, where God seems silent, don't assume something's wrong with you. Don't rush to force a move just to feel productive.

Spiritual Warfare: Building Your Battle Plan

God may be teaching you the discipline of restraint, training you to trust His timing more than your urgency, His plan more than your hustle.

Waiting on God is one of the strongest stands you'll ever take.

Facing Forward, But Not Charging Ahead

God isn't in a hurry. He's building something in you that haste would ruin. The lessons of stillness aren't just for this season. They are preparation for every season ahead.

You may not see dramatic changes yet. Things might still feel quiet, uncertain, or even slow. But you are being prepared. Your heart is being turned more fully toward Him. Your ear is being trained to hear His voice clearly above all the noise.

When that time comes to move, you'll know it. Not because the attack pushed you into it or because impatience finally won. But because the Spirit led you with that settled peace that only He gives.

That's where the real victory is won.

9

BUILD YOUR BATTLE PLAN

THE SPIRIT

You know those moments in the fight when the attacks build up that all you want to do is something, *anything*, to make it stop. You feel the urge to fix it, confront it, decide it, or just push through in your own strength.

The greatest danger in this war isn't always fear, temptation, or even failure. Sometimes it's getting ahead of God. The enemy loves to prod you into acting before God speaks, because the moment you step out of position, you're fighting on ground he can control.

Purpose of This Battle Plan

The purpose of this battle plan is to train you to obey God's direction in real time, so you don't mistake pressure for leading, and you don't mistake stillness for failure.

This plan is designed to help you:
- Identify when you feel rushed, driven, or pushed to act.
- Separate a God-given burden from self-driven urgency.
- Practice restraint when the Spirit.
- Move with clean obedience when God says to go.

Step 1: Name the "Pressure to Move"

There is a moment in almost every battle when the enemy stops trying to make you quit and starts trying to make you rush. You feel it in your chest. You feel it in your thoughts. You start saying, *"I have to do something now."*

Action:

Write down the situation where you feel the strongest attack:

1. The situation:

2. Now check what your attack sounds like:

   ☐ *"If I don't act now, it'll get worse."*

   ☐ *"If I really cared, I would do something immediately."*

   ☐ *"If I wait, I'm being irresponsible."*

   ☐ *"If I don't fix this, nobody will."*

   ☐ *"God is taking too long—so I have to move."*

   ☐ Other:

Step 2: Separate Burden from Permission

A burden can be real, and still God has not given you a green light to move. A need can be urgent, yet not yours to carry or fix. This is where so many believers fall short. They confuse concern with command, feeling with direction, and heartache with a call to act right now.

Action:

Look at the situation you named in **Step 1**.
Complete these honestly and bluntly.

1. What I want to do:

2. Why I want to do it (be blunt):
    - ☐ to stop the discomfort
    - ☐ to get control back
    - ☐ to prove I'm being faithful
    - ☐ to quiet people's opinions
    - ☐ to end the waiting
    - ☐ other:

3. Now write one sentence:

    "Lord, I feel the burden of _____, but I do not want to move without Your direction."

Step 3: Run the "Spirit or Pressure?"

You feel the push to act. Your heart is racing, your mind is loud, and everything in you says, *"Do something now."* But before you move, you have to test where that push is coming from.

God's leading brings settled clarity, even when it's hard. Pressure brings frantic urgency, even when it feels right. The Holy Spirit will never drive you to step around what God has already said in His Word. He won't rush you into sin, compromise, or self-reliance.

Action:

Look at the situation and the step you feel pushed toward. Answer these honestly in writing. No rushing.

1. Does the step I want to take violate Scripture?

    ☐ Yes
    ☐ No
    ☐ Not sure

    If yes/not sure, explain:

2. When I pray and slow down, does the urge get clearer and calmer or louder and more frantic?

    ☐ clearer + calmer
    ☐ louder + more frantic

    Write what you're noticing:

3. Is this pulling me toward God... or offering quick relief from discomfort?

    ☐ toward God
    ☐ toward relief

    Explain:

4. Right now, after running this test, I believe God is calling me to:

    ☐ WAIT and hold position.
    ☐ MOVE in obedience.
    ☐ SEEK COUNSEL because I'm not clear.

    Explain:

Step 4: If God Says "Wait..."

Waiting is not doing nothing. Waiting is obedience with restraint. It is staying submitted when your flesh wants to sprint ahead and take control.

If the test in Step 3 pointed to wait, this step is your plan to obey without drifting.

Action:

Write your *"hold position"* plan:

1. What does faithful waiting look like for me this week?
(Examples: daily prayer, serving where you are, keeping your heart right, doing the next clear duty God has already given you.)

2. What will I not do while I wait?
(Examples: forcing conversations, manipulating outcomes, making fear-driven decisions, researching every possible solution late at night.)

3. When the urge to rush hits, I will do this first:

    ☐ Stop and pray for 60 seconds
    ☐ Open my Bible before I open my phone
    ☐ Write the decision down and wait 24 hours
    ☐ Ask a mature believer for counsel
    ☐ Other:

    Explain:

4. Write one sentence you will say out loud when the attacks start: *(Start with the example if it fits, or make it your own.)* "I will not move without orders. I will obey God by waiting."

    My sentence:

Step 5: If God Says "Go."

When God does give clear direction, you don't need to hype yourself up or work up the courage. You don't need to panic or rush ahead in fear. You move with simple obedience—steady, trusting, one step at a time.

If the test pointed to move, this step is your plan to obey without adding your own drama or delay.

Action:
Write your *"go"* orders. Be specific and honest.

1. The step God is telling me to take:

2. When I will do it (date/time):

3. Who I will inform/ask to pray:

4. What obedience will cost me (be honest):

5. Now write your one-sentence commitment:

    "Lord, because You have spoken, I will obey You by _____
    _____*."*

Step 6: Choose Your Anchor Verse.

You need one Scripture to return to when your emotions start demanding action. Pick one that fits your current battle (waiting, restraint, direction, peace).

Action:

Write one verse (or short passage) fully, word for word (KJV):

_____

10

THE MISSION OF THE ARMY

Learning to fight together for kingdom ground.

You've come a long way through these pages, and if you're still here, it means the Lord is doing something real in your heart. You've learned to recognize the enemy's attacks when they hit: those sudden waves of exhaustion, the emotions that rise without reason, and the financial pressures that seem perfectly timed to shake your faith. You've taken hold of God's weapons, put on His armor piece by piece, and started building those daily habits of prayer and truth that help you stand when the battle rages fiercely.

But here's the truth many believers miss:
The fight was never meant to end with you just surviving.

God saved you for something greater than holding your ground alone. He's preparing you for the mission, shaping your personal endurance into something that strengthens others. I've seen this happen in lives right in our church.

Spiritual Warfare: Building Your Battle Plan

There was a young man named Mike who got saved in the middle of chaos. He lost his job, his family was falling apart, and everything was crumbling. For months, his walk with God was pure survival. He showed up to church, clung to his Bible, and prayed through every attack just to make it through the day. That season built real strength in him, the kind you only get in the fire. But then something changed. He started noticing the brother sitting next to him, fighting similar battles. Mike opened up, shared what God had taught him, and soon they were praying together, holding each other accountable. Mike wasn't just surviving anymore. He was helping carry someone else's load.

That's the shift God brings.

Your obedience has to start personally. It always does. You learn to follow Him when no one sees, resist temptation when you feel alone on the battlefield, and walk the narrow path even when it costs you. God doesn't leave you there forever. He widens the circle. He starts positioning you to carry weight with others, turning what began as your private endurance into shared responsibility.

The Bible describes this as the mark of growing maturity, when we move from needing milk to handling solid food, from basic survival to faithful stewardship (Hebrews 5:12–14). The warfare doesn't ease up. Attacks still come hard and fast. But your perspective changes. You stop reacting only to what's hitting you and start hearing what God is doing in the bigger fight. You realize obedience was never meant to stop with your own life. It's designed to flow through you to the people around you.

God isn't raising up scattered survivors who barely hold on by themselves. He's forming an army.

Scripture tells us we are many members in one body, placed exactly where He wants us, not by chance, but with divine purpose (1 Corinthians 12:18). In spiritual warfare, strength doesn't come from running faster or fighting harder on your own. It comes from tight formation, ranks locked together so the front holds strong. The call forward isn't *"Charge alone."* It's "Stay in the place I've set you, and advance when I give the order."

Chapter 10: The Mission of the Army

This shift changes the questions you ask. It moves you from *"How do I make it through this attack?"* to *"What has God entrusted us to carry together?"* Kingdom ground isn't secured by lone resolve, no matter how sincere. It's preserved through ordered obedience, everyone standing in their post, watching each other's backs. We're called stewards of God's mysteries, and real faithfulness isn't freelance or unanchored. It's bound to something greater than your personal assignment (1 Corinthians 4:1–2). Miss this, and you'll drift. You'll keep fighting like the battle rests entirely on your shoulders, and that kind of isolation narrows everything: your vision, your discernment, and your patience. It drains you faster than you realize.

When strength is shared in formation, it holds longer and goes further, just as Scripture promises that *"two are better than one... and a threefold cord is not quickly broken"* (Ecclesiastes 4:9–12).

God has always moved His people as one—one Lord, one body, one calling (Ephesians 4:4–6). Those quiet lessons of waiting and restraint you learned in solitary seasons aren't left behind. They expand, becoming the steady posture that supports the whole line. Your obedience stops being only about your path and starts upholding what God is building through everyone around you.

He's building something real, something lasting. And He's placing you right in the middle of it.

You don't abandon personal faithfulness—that's still the foundation. But you begin to see how it gains its full power in formation. This isn't about frantic activity or pushing ahead out of urgency. It's about readiness, together.

God isn't just forming individual soldiers. He's forming a people.

So let me ask you today. Are you still fighting like the battle is yours alone? Or are you locking shields with the brothers and sisters God has placed around you?

Spiritual Warfare: Building Your Battle Plan

From Surviving to Serving Together

From the very beginning, God has never sent His people into battle without a clear structure. His commands come ordered. His presence is marked by discipline. Think of the tabernacle in the wilderness, carefully arranged exactly as He directed, every tribe in its place, every detail purposeful. That same design carries right into the local church today. It isn't random. It isn't merely traditional. It's deliberate, governed, and purposeful. The Bible declares, *"For God is not the author of confusion, but of peace..."* and all things should be done decently and in order (1 Corinthians 14:33, 40).

The local church isn't an optional add-on to your Christian life, something you join when it's convenient. It's God's ordained formation for the spiritual fight.

When pressure mounts and attacks intensify, the church is where your patience is preserved, and your strength is multiplied. God placed gifts within the body, teachers, shepherds, leaders, not to spotlight personalities, but to equip the saints, build up the whole, and anchor the weary when the battle stretches long (Ephesians 4:11–16). That's why Scripture calls the church the pillar and ground of the truth (1 Timothy 3:15).

Spiritual warfare tests more than personal conviction. It tests formation.

Even sincere believers can drift when structure weakens, discernment fades, endurance cracks, and direction blurs. I've watched it happen with a sister named Sarah. She loved the Lord. But when her marriage fell apart, and her kids started rebelling, she pulled back. She thought she'd just pray at home, keep things private, and handle it between her and God. Her heart was right. She wasn't angry at the church. She just felt too raw to be around people. Without the steadying structure of church life, sound preaching, faithful counsel, and brothers and sisters locking shields around her, the attacks wore her down in ways she didn't expect. Isolation made the lies louder. The weight felt heavier.

Chapter 10: The Mission of the Army

God didn't call her to fight alone. He called her back into formation, where others could help carry the load. And when she stepped back in, healing started in ways solitude never could have produced.

God sets every member in the body as it pleases Him (1 Corinthians 12:18). That placement isn't optional; it's how care flows, protection works, and the entire body absorbs the blows together (1 Corinthians 12:25–26).

Growth was never designed to happen alone. Neither does spiritual maturity develop in isolation. Soldiers are trained together, moving in ranks together, obeying as one unified unit.

The church isn't a stage to display your personal growth. It's the place where your growth is forged, through sound doctrine that anchors truth, spiritual authority that aligns direction, and shared responsibility that shields the whole.

No genuine path to biblical maturity bypasses the local church.

This isn't about controlling you. It's about protecting you. Spiritual authority isn't a threat to your freedom. It's defense against deception that often leads you right into another attack. Biblical leadership doesn't hinder God's work. It preserves it when chaos threatens to tear the church apart. And doctrine isn't a burden. It's an anchor in the storm.

God fights through order, not confusion. That's why pastors are charged to watch for souls as those who must give account (Hebrews 13:17) and to shepherd with vigilance against the wolves that will come (Acts 20:28–31).

Deception often creeps in quietly. A believer says, "*I can worship God anywhere, without the church.*" On the surface, it sounds spiritual, after all, worship isn't confined to a building. But warfare isn't that simple. When devotion is detached from oversight and private faith stands apart from shared authority, it may feel free, but it leaves you vulnerable.

**You're not openly rebelling.
You're just exposed.**

Spiritual Warfare: Building Your Battle Plan

I've counseled believers who started drifting this way. They loved the Lord. They read their Bible at home, listened to sermons online, and prayed in private. They told themselves, *"I don't need the structure. I'm fine on my own."* At first it felt liberating. No schedules. No messy people. No accountability that rubbed them wrong.

Over time, the attacks found the gaps. Lies went unchallenged because no one was speaking truth into their life. Discernment dulled because no pastor was watching over their soul. Temptation grew stronger because no brother or sister was locking shields beside them. What started as *"freedom"* turned into isolation, and isolation turned into real spiritual danger.

The enemy doesn't only tempt you with open sin. He hunts the isolated. The Bible warns us, *"Be sober, be vigilant; because your adversary the devil, as a roaring lion, walketh about, seeking whom he may devour"* (1 Peter 5:8). Lions don't charge the whole herd head-on. They wait. They watch. They target the one that strays, the one that lags behind, the one that wanders off alone.

Scripture confirms the danger and the remedy: two are better than one, and a threefold cord is not easily broken (Ecclesiastes 4:9–12).

Real spiritual strength isn't self-made.
It's multiplied through connection.

The church isn't primarily for emotional uplift or weekly encouragement. It's where truth is preached, doctrine guarded, and disciples shaped. Those elements aren't extras. They're essential for battle.

That's where deception gets exposed before it takes root. That's where direction is clarified when your own eyes are clouded. That's where the crushing weight of life is shared so no one collapses alone.

When those are missing, even the sincerest heart can falter.

Pastoral care isn't administrative busywork. It's frontline defense. Sound doctrine isn't dry and academic. It stabilizes you when everything else is chaos. Oversight isn't optional control. It's protective covering when attacks come hard.

Chapter 10: The Mission of the Army

False teachers scatter and draw away followers (Acts 20:29–31). Maturity means no longer being children tossed to and fro by every wind of doctrine (Ephesians 4:14).

God has left us in the battle, but never to fight it alone.

The local church isn't a break from responsibility. It's where responsibility is carried rightly. It's not a substitute for obedience, it's where obedience is formed and sustained. It's not a side activity. It's the central structure where mature soldiers are forged.

Believers are fitly framed together as a dwelling place for God's Spirit (Ephesians 2:21–22), and growth comes through the supply of every joint and band (Colossians 2:19).

Are you isolated right now? Are you carrying the fight alone because church feels messy, distant, or unnecessary?

The lion is watching. Get back in the herd!

Why God Made Us to Carry Each Other

God never intended for any of us to endure spiritual attacks in isolation. From Genesis to Revelation, Scripture shows strength being shared among His people, not because personal responsibility isn't enough, but because one perspective is limited, especially when the battle presses hard (Romans 1:11–12; 1 Corinthians 12:21). *"There is a way which seemeth right unto a man, but the end thereof are the ways of death"* (Proverbs 14:12). That built-in limitation isn't a flaw in us. It's part of God's wise design, creating a structure of dependence that protects through connection.

This is where isolation becomes truly dangerous. It rarely announces itself as rebellion. More often it feels reasonable, even discerning. It can look like maturity, sound like depth, and be framed as wisdom. Yet a believer who loves the Lord, trusts His presence, and sincerely wants to obey can gradually step outside God's protective design during intense attack. God hasn't abandoned them, but His intended structure is bypassed, leaving the soul exposed in ways that are hard to recognize at first.

Spiritual Warfare: Building Your Battle Plan

We have the promise that *"I will never leave thee, nor forsake thee"* (Hebrews 13:5). But that promise was never meant to replace the clear command *"not to forsake the assembling of ourselves together..."* (Hebrews 10:25). God's strength isn't limited to private moments, it's revealed powerfully in community, through encouragement, correction, and protection that grow stronger as conflict intensifies.

This is how God builds patience and sharpens discernment: lives joined together, walking side by side under the same authority and governed by the same truth. Nourishment and growth flow when we stay connected to Christ the Head and to one another (Colossians 2:19). Blind spots aren't removed in solitude, they're revealed and healed in close proximity.

God doesn't call us to abandon personal responsibility. He calls us to carry it together. *"Bear ye one another's burdens, and so fulfil the law of Christ"* (Galatians 6:2). Shared strength doesn't weaken accountability, it stabilizes it. Alone, strain multiplies and vision narrows. Shared, clarity holds and our patience steadies.

That's why accountability matters so much in spiritual warfare, not as control or suspicion, but as shared vigilance. Under heavy strain, discernment needs more than individual wisdom. It needs protection. Accountability provides that by placing decisions within relationships where perspective widens and truth is spoken in love (Ephesians 4:15). When pressure rises, judgment can compress quickly, but shared life slows that process and keeps space for truth to breathe. Discernment is too precious to be left unguarded.

Here's the beautiful paradox: vulnerability inside God's design isn't risk, it's the strongest protection against deception. It doesn't replace personal obedience. It supports and strengthens it. Shared life keeps the light on the things that need exposing (Ephesians 5:13), especially when darkness starts whispering lies.

This shared strength builds directly on the restraint and waiting you've already learned. Obedience under prolonged pressure was never meant to be sustained alone. Paul urged believers to *"stand fast in one spirit, with one mind striving together for the faith of the gospel"* (Philippians 1:27). That kind of alignment doesn't just

Chapter 10: The Mission of the Army

maintain your posture, it preserves your direction and ensures you're not standing alone when the full weight hits.

God preserves clarity in the battle not by isolating His people, but by forming them tightly together.

The Tools God Put in the Church for the Fight

When the battle drags on longer than expected, when the enemy refuses to retreat, and obedience starts feeling more like a question than a certainty, God hasn't left us to guess our way forward. He hasn't called us to grow in confusion. From the beginning, His design has been intentional and ordered: *"Let all things be done decently and in order"* (1 Corinthians 14:40). That order isn't cold or rigid. It's deliberate care that matures us even in the heat of conflict.

It all starts with **salvation**, the moment a soul passes from death to life and becomes a new creature in Christ (John 5:24; 2 Corinthians 5:17). That's the beginning, not the end.

Baptism follows as the first clear step of obedience, a public declaration that says, *"I belong to Him, and I'm standing with His people."* The Great Commission makes it clear: baptism isn't optional (Matthew 28:19–20). It's the God-ordained threshold into visible alignment.

I've seen it over and over, sincere believers hungry for truth, eager to grow and walk in victory, yet something stalls because they never take that step of baptism.

They aren't stubborn or defiant. They just haven't followed through. If you want to go deeper in your relationship with Christ, follow Him in believer's baptism. That's where intention turns into action, and preparation and growth truly begin.

From there, discipleship takes root, not a quick program you finish, but a lifelong process of formation and training. Jesus didn't say, *"Just get them saved."* He commanded us to teach new believers to observe everything He taught (Matthew 28:20). The early church lived this out, continuing steadfastly in the apostles' doctrine and

Spiritual Warfare: Building Your Battle Plan

fellowship (Acts 2:42). It wasn't casual or seasonal. It was anchored, gritty obedience that held even when war raged around them.

These are the instruments God has placed in the church, not checkboxes to mark off, but living provisions to preserve clarity and build endurance when obedience costs you dearly.

- **Discipleship** comes through steady teaching, real relationships, honest questions, shared prayer, loving correction, and wise counsel. We're able to admonish one another because God's Word thoroughly equips us for every good work (Romans 15:14; 2 Timothy 3:16–17). It's not always fast, but it's faithful, training us not just for peaceful days, but for obedience under fire.

- **Accountability** belongs here too, not as surveillance or suspicion, but as mutual protection and shared vigilance. It guards your discernment when stress clouds judgment. That's why we're told to exhort one another daily and restore the fallen in meekness (Hebrews 3:13; Galatians 6:1). It's shepherding, not control.

- **Biblical counseling** steps in when sin, sorrow, or suffering has knocked you off balance. It's not pop psychology or clinical labels, it's godly care that helps you hear the Spirit's voice again through the Word, bringing clarity rooted in truth.

- **Pastoral oversight** stands alongside, where shepherds guard, feed, and guide the flock under pressure. Pastors are charged to take heed to the whole flock and watch for souls, knowing battles wear the mind down, and doctrine can blur when flesh drifts (Acts 20:28; Hebrews 13:17). A shepherd doesn't lord over the sheep. He watches like a faithful watchman.

I've seen a brother transformed by this kind of care. He came in carrying years of hidden struggle, shame keeping him silent. He tried

Chapter 10: The Mission of the Army

fighting alone for so long. But when he finally opened up in counseling, let the Word search him, submitted to pastoral oversight and real accountability, the chains started breaking. Today he's standing strong, discipling others, because those tools did their work.

And then there is **united prayer**, not just private communion, but the church lifting one voice together. The early believers gathered with one accord, and their unified cry moved heaven (Acts 1:14; 4:24). That kind of prayer isn't formality, it's a weapon that reminds us strength comes not from within, but from the God we call on as one.

These instruments aren't accessories to the Christian life. They're God's own tools for formation in the fight.

They shelter more than they bind, reinforce more than they restrict. Through them, God keeps us from mistaking independence for maturity.

Safety is found in a multitude of counselors (Proverbs 11:14), and shepherds lead not as lords, but as examples to the flock (1 Peter 5:3). These provisions shape lives that stay steady under pressure, obedient in the fire, aligned with truth, and ready when God finally says, "*Go.*"

The Real Danger of Fighting Alone

Isolation almost never feels like outright rebellion. More often it feels reasonable, even careful. A believer quietly pulls back, not angry, not defiant, just trying to protect themselves or simplify things. It can feel strong, even mature. For a while, it seems to work; they carry the weight, stay faithful in private. But slowly, almost imperceptibly, something shifts.

Scripture warns against exactly this kind of quiet drift, not loud sin, but gradual slipping away (Hebrews 2:1). "*There is a way which seemeth right unto a man, but the end thereof are the ways of death*" (Proverbs 14:12).

Isolation is dangerous because it reshapes how you think under attack.

Spiritual Warfare: Building Your Battle Plan

When you carry heavy attacks alone, decisions come from a narrowed viewpoint. You're doing your best, but your understanding goes untested and unchallenged. That is when your discernment wears thin. God never intended believers to face spiritual attacks in isolation, which is why He provides counsel and encouragement through the local church (Hebrews 3:13), where safety is found in godly counsel—not because we are weak, but because the attack is real (Proverbs 11:14).

Lone-wolf Christianity is when a believer decides to leave the church and worship God on their own terms. It looks spiritual from the outside. It can even involve prayer, worship, and a sincere effort to obey God. But when the believer leaves the church, even with the best of intentions, they step outside God's design for protection and become exposed to the enemy.

God's Word commands us to *"not to forsake the assembling of ourselves together..."* and this command goes far beyond simply showing up to a service. The gathering of the church is God's design for our spiritual protection. In Hebrews 10:24–25, we are reminded that we need one another to provoke love, encourage faithfulness, and guard our hearts from drifting in isolation. When believers remove themselves from regular fellowship, they don't just miss a service—they step outside a God-given safeguard for their walk with Christ.

There are seasons when you need to withdraw alone with God. Jesus often did (Mark 1:35; Luke 5:16). The danger isn't being alone. It's stepping outside God-ordained structure and facing the fight unprotected.

What many believers miss is that God deliberately places each of us into the church (1 Corinthians 12:18) and calls us to walk under spiritual authority.

I've seen this danger hit close to home in our church. There was a sister who loved the Lord with all her heart. She served, she gave, and she prayed often. But when something hurtful happened at church, she started pulling back. Not in anger. Just quietly. *"I'll keep my faith at home for a while,"* she thought. It felt wise. It felt protective. She still read her Bible, she still prayed, but she worshiped alone. Month after month, the attacks began to build up. Lies she used to spot easily started feeling true. Temptations grew heavier. Her ability to clearly

Chapter 10: The Mission of the Army

discern situations began to dull. By the time she reached out, she was exhausted, confused, drifting farther than she ever intended. When she returned to the church and reconciled with her sisters, her strength returned, and she was able to stand again.

Fight alone long enough, and your own thoughts begin defining your reality.

The mind becomes both the command center and the battlefield, with no outside voice to correct it. Even sincere faith can slowly drift when a believer removes themselves from regular fellowship, making it harder to discern what is true and what is a lie. The heart convinces itself that everything is fine, yet Scripture warns us that *"the heart is deceitful above all things"* (Jeremiah 17:9).

If you are out of church, fighting alone doesn't mean you've failed. It means you're carrying more than God ever intended you to carry, without the support He already provided. True spiritual maturity isn't doing everything yourself—it's growing together, letting others hold the line with you when you're under attack.

The church grows when it is fitly joined together, supplying strength through every joint (Ephesians 4:16). We are nourished and knit together through those connections (Colossians 2:19). Two are better than one, and a threefold cord is not quickly broken (Ecclesiastes 4:9–12).

Isolated believers often don't stop caring. They care deeply, sometimes too much, but they carry it alone.

That's what wears them out and turns what seems like manageable attacks into a real nightmare. God always provides protection through the church and makes a way for each one of us to stand (1 Corinthians 10:13).

Locked In and Ready

Before God ever moves His people out of stillness, He prepares them first. That preparation is rarely just physical. It's spiritual. Long before

Spiritual Warfare: Building Your Battle Plan

there is a call to move, God is doing work beneath the surface.

That's why Scripture calls us to *"stand fast in one spirit, with one mind striving together for the faith of the gospel..."* (Philippians 1:27). That kind of standing assumes alignment. It assumes that God's people are facing the same direction, aiming for the same goal, and moving with the same heart. God works through those who are steady and unified, not through individual urgency pulling in different directions.

And that matters, because God *"is not the author of confusion, but of peace..."* (1 Corinthians 14:33). The church doesn't advance on raw energy or individual works. When believers aren't unified under the same truth, direction, and authority, we wear out and begin to fall apart.

We see this pattern throughout Scripture. In the wilderness, Israel didn't march whenever they felt ready. They moved when God moved. If the cloud stayed, they stayed. If it lifted, they followed (Numbers 9:17–23). In waiting, God renewed their strength (Isaiah 40:31).

Nothing about that principle has changed. The church doesn't move forward because everyone does what seems right in their own eyes. It moves when God gives clear direction, and He gives that direction through formation. That's why He provided leaders to equip and prepare His people before the work begins (Ephesians 4). And that's why, in the upper room, power didn't fall simply because people were eager. It fell because they were in one accord, sharing the same heart and obedience (Acts 2).

I've seen believers sense a genuine burden, feel a real call, and rush ahead with good intentions. Ministries were started, changes were pushed, words were spoken—all because the need felt urgent. But without alignment in the body, without shared direction, those efforts often fizzled or caused unnecessary division.

Then I've seen the opposite. A sister sensed God stirring something new in her heart. Instead of running ahead, she brought it to her pastor. She shared it with her small group. She waited for confirmation. And when the church aligned around it, the fruit was abundant and lasting. God blessed what was birthed in unity.

That's the picture God wants us to see. His people advance only when alignment is solid. That's why this chapter isn't urging you to

Chapter 10: The Mission of the Army

rush out and act on your own. Just because you sense the next step doesn't mean you're meant to take it *solo*. This isn't a call to move faster. It's a call to hold your ground until the whole body is ready.

God's goal for you isn't personal initiative apart from others. It's shared obedience.

We're told not to lean on our own understanding but to acknowledge Him in all our ways, trusting He will direct our path (Proverbs 3:5–6). The church moves not by instinct, but by formation that holds and protects true direction.

You've learned how to stand personally, and that foundation matters deeply. But now you're not standing alone. The next move isn't about what you alone understand, it's about what we're called to carry together as the body of Christ.

God has placed every believer where He wants them, fitly joined so every joint supplies strength (Ephesians 4:16; 1 Corinthians 12:18). That placement isn't for status. It's for power in battle. The battle plan always follows posture, and counsel comes before advance (Proverbs 20:18).

So for now, hold your ground. Stay in formation. Remain under the authority God has given. Stay connected to the people He's placed around you.

"Can two walk together, except they be agreed?" (Amos 3:3). "Wait on the LORD… and he shall strengthen thine heart" (Psalm 27:14).

What God is establishing here is posture and formation, solid alignment that must be in place before any unified advance can be faithful and strong.

"*Stand fast in the Lord*" (Philippians 4:1).

And when it's not yet time to charge, "*stand still,*" and let God give the next step (Exodus 14:13).

If you're reading this and you're not under the authority and care of a local church, it's time to change that today.

You don't need a perfect church, none exist. You need a biblical one, where the Word is preached without compromise, authority is

Spiritual Warfare: Building Your Battle Plan

honored, and obedience is trained not just in easy times but when the battle is fierce.

> **Find a church that holds the line.**
> **Join the formation.**

DON'T FIGHT ALONE ANYMORE!

10

BUILD YOUR BATTLE PLAN

THE MISSION

You know how exhausting it feels to fight alone. The attack comes, the pressure builds, and you're holding the line by yourself—praying hard, standing on truth, guarding your mind. You endure for a while, but deep down there's this weariness, this sense that something's missing.

Up to this point, we've focused on how you endure attacks, how you guard your mind, how you stand firm when the battle drags on. Those are vital. But now the Lord is shifting your focus. This isn't about surviving the fight in isolation anymore. It's about learning to stay in formation, to carry responsibility alongside others, and to remain spiritually aligned inside the body God has placed you in.

Purpose of This Battle Plan

The purpose of this battle plan is to train you to stop fighting as an isolated believer and to step fully into God's design for shared obedience and collective strength.

This battle plan is designed to help you:

- Recognize where you have been carrying the fight alone instead of within God's ordained structure.
- Identify tendencies toward isolation that weaken protection and invite unnecessary pressure.
- Commit intentionally to alignment, accountability, and obedience within the local church.
- Prepare your heart to move only when God gives direction — together, not independently.

Step 1: Identify Where You've Been Fighting Alone

Spiritual isolation rarely announces itself as rebellion or sin. Most of the time, it grows quietly out of pressure, fatigue, disappointment, or just plain self-reliance. You don't stop loving God or trusting His Word. You just start carrying more of the fight by yourself than He ever intended.

Before you can move forward in formation, you need to be honest about where you've been standing alone.

Action:

Answer the following honestly.

1. Check any that apply to you right now:

    ☐ I tend to withdraw when I'm under spiritual attack.
    ☐ I handle battles privately instead of asking for help.
    ☐ I avoid accountability because it feels uncomfortable.
    ☐ I've minimized the role of the local church in my spiritual life.
    ☐ I've convinced myself I'm *"fine on my own."*

2. Now write one sentence: *"In this season, I have been carrying the fight alone by _____."*

Step 2: Acknowledge God's Design for Protection

You feel the weight when the battle drags on, don't you? The temptation is to pull back, handle it quietly, prove you can stand on your own. But God never designed you to be sustained in isolation. When the attack increases, His protection increases through the structure He gave—the local church, its authority, its shared responsibility. Resisting that design doesn't make you stronger or more spiritual. It leaves you exposed, more vulnerable than you realize.

This step is about agreeing with God's design, even when it challenges your preference for privacy or self-reliance.

Action:

Complete the sentences below slowly and deliberately.

"God did not design me to fight spiritual battles _____

_____."

"According to Scripture, strength and protection increase when I ___

_____."

Now write one truth you must accept, even if it challenges your comfort:

"I need the church because _____

_____."

Step 3: Commit to Staying in Formation

Formation requires submission, not blind obedience or surrendering your mind, but willing alignment under the God-given authority He has placed in the local church. This is where many believers hesitate. It's not usually because they don't trust God. It's because past wounds make church feel unsafe, fear whispers that submission will cost too much, or pride says, *"I can handle this on my own."*

But alignment is not loss of freedom. It is protection in battle. It's the place where the enemy's schemes are exposed faster, where burdens are shared, and where God's authority flows to cover you.

Action:

Answer the following clearly.

"Right now, my relationship to the local church can best be described as _____*."*

Explain:

Now write one specific commitment:

"I commit to remaining connected and accountable by _____
_____*."*

Say it out loud when you finish. This isn't about perfection. It's about stepping back into the place God designed for your protection and strength. The body needs you, and you need the body. Take this step. The Lord will meet you there.

Step 4: Identify Who You Will Lock Shields With

No soldier stands in formation without knowing exactly who is on his left and on his right. You can't fight together if you don't know who's beside you, ready to cover your blind spot and trusting you to cover theirs.

Shared obedience isn't vague friendship. It's intentional relationships where truth can be spoken in love, burdens can be carried together, and discernment can be protected. This isn't about oversharing with everyone or dumping your struggles on the whole church. It's about shared vigilance with the people God has already placed near you.

Action:

Write the name(s) of at least one person God has placed in your life for spiritual support. It might be a pastor, a small group leader, a mature brother or sister, a mentor. Be specific.

Name(s):

Now write one sentence committing to reach out instead of retreating:

"When the attack increases, I will not isolate. I will reach out to _____."

Explain:

Step 5: Align Your Movement with God's Timing

Formation always comes before advance. You can feel the burden, sense the calling, even know the right thing to do. But if you step out alone or ahead of God's timing, you create exposure the enemy is quick to exploit.

God's power flows strongest when His people move together, under His direction. Waiting for that alignment isn't weakness or inaction. It's wisdom. It's trust. It's the way victories are won without unnecessary wounds.

This final step trains you to wait, listen, and move only when God gives direction—together, not independently.

Action:

Complete the following statements as a prayerful commitment.

"Before I act, I will seek confirmation through _____ _____."

"If God says wait, I will _____."

"If God says move, I will move _____ _____."

Now write one Scripture you will stand on when impatience or urgency pressures you to act alone:

PART FOUR

THE FINAL BATTLE PLAN

*The war is ongoing,
but your orders are clear.*

11

YOUR FINAL BATTLE PLAN

Your Personalized Strategy for Spiritual Victory

Congratulations, you did it! You've reached the final step—not the end of the fight, but the place where everything you've learned comes together. The chapters behind you were training. They helped you understand the nature of spiritual warfare, how the enemy works, and how God equips His people to stand. What follows is not new instruction. It is the application of what you already know.

This Battle Plan is not something you complete once and set aside. It is a practical tool to use when the pressure is real. When confusion, heaviness, or resistance rises, you need clarity instead of panic. You do not need to fill out every section every time. Begin with the first question and follow the instructions given as you complete it.

This plan is meant to be used, returned to, and relied upon. It is not about perfection or completion. It is about standing firm in Christ, walking in obedience, and holding the ground God has given you.

THE FINAL BATTLE PLAN
Standing Firm Under Spiritual Attack

This Battle Plan is designed for use when you are under spiritual pressure. Begin where the pressure is greatest, follow the direction given, and return as needed.

Are you 100% certain that you belong to Jesus Christ and that your salvation is secure?

☐ Yes, I have placed my trust and faith in Jesus Christ.
☐ I am unsure and need to settle this before going further.

If you're not sure, pause here and review *Chapter 1: Before You Fight, You Must Belong*. This entire Battle Plan relies on the assurance that you belong to Him.

When doubt or accusation rises, I will remind myself:

What is true about me:	Scripture I will stand on:
☐ I am forgiven.	☐ Ephesians 1:7
☐ I am accepted.	☐ Ephesians 1:6
☐ I am secure in Christ.	☐ John 10:28
☐ I am not condemned.	☐ Romans 8:1

What happened?

Briefly describe the situation you are dealing with right now. (An event, conversation, decision, temptation, pressure, or season)

Where do you feel the possible attack is right now?

☐ Mind (thoughts, confusion, doubt, racing or foggy thinking).
☐ Emotions (fear, sadness, anger, heaviness).
☐ Body (fatigue, sickness, tension, restlessness).
☐ Relationships (conflict, offense, isolation, division).
☐ Finances (stress, fear of provision, instability).
☐ Spiritual focus (dryness, resistance to prayer or Scripture).

How many areas (above) are affected?

☐ 1-2 Areas (possibly not a spiritual attack).
☐ 3-6 Areas (possibly a spiritual attack).

How am I responding right now?

☐ I prayed and brought this to the Lord.
☐ I reacted emotionally.
☐ I ignored it and tried to push through.
☐ I withdrew or isolated.
☐ I became defensive or angry.
☐ I sought counsel or encouragement.
☐ I tried to fix it in my own strength.
☐ I'm not sure how I responded.

Use the guide below to determine your next move.

☐ My response has been unclear or inconsistent
→ Go to Chapter 3 - Step 1: Call Out the Attack.

☐ My response has been reactive, emotional, or self-directed
→ Go to Chapter 3 - Step 2: Turn to God Immediately

☐ My response has been submitted to God first.
→ continue forward in the Battle Plan.

What Bible verse am I standing on right now?

(Write the complete verse below.)

Write a short prayer giving this attack to the Lord?

Am I remaining connected to the local church right now?

☐ Yes, I am faithfully attending and staying connected.
☐ No, I have pulled back or missed consistently.
☐ I am present but disengaged or drifting.

Use the guide below to determine your next move.

☐ If I have pulled back or disengaged
→ Go to Chapter 3 – Step 3: Stay Connected and Hold the Line

☐ If I am faithfully connected
→ Continue forward in the Battle Plan.

Am I giving the enemy any continued access?

☐ Unconfessed sin.
☐ Bitterness or unforgiveness.
☐ Ongoing conflict not addressed.
☐ Prayerlessness or neglect of Scripture.
☐ Compromise in habits, media, or influences.
☐ Isolation from godly fellowship.
☐ Pride or resistance to correction.
☐ Fear controlling decisions.
☐ I'm not sure yet.

Use the guide below to determine your next move.

☐ I see one or more areas that may be open
→ Go to Chapter 4 – Step 1: Identify the Open Door

☐ I am unsure and need clarity
→ Go to Chapter 4 – Step 2: Ask the Lord to Reveal What Needs to Be Closed

☐ No clear doors are open, but pressure remains
→ Go to Chapter 4 – Step 3: Strengthen the Wall and Stay Alert

Where is the battleground right now?

Check the area where the conflict is being fought, not just felt.

☐ Thought life
→ Go to Chapter 5 – Battleground of the Mind

☐ Desires / temptation
→ Go to Chapter 5 – Battleground of the Flesh

☐ Relationships / influence
→ Go to Chapter 5 – Battleground of Influence

☐ Fear / uncertainty about the future
→ Go to Chapter 5 – Battleground of Trust

☐ Multiple areas
→ Begin with Chapter 5 – Battleground of the Mind

What weapons am I actively using right now?

Check what you are actually using, not what you believe in.

☐ Scripture (spoken, read, or recalled)
→ Go to Chapter 6 – The Weapon of God's Word

☐ Prayer
→ Go to Chapter 6 – The Weapon of Dependence

☐ Fellowship / counsel
→ Go to Chapter 6 – The Weapon of Community

☐ Confession and repentance
→ Go to Chapter 6 – The Weapon of Light

☐ I am not actively using any weapons
→ Stop here and begin with prayer and Scripture

Is my armor in place right now?

Check any area that feels weakened or neglected.

☐ Truth (clarity vs lies)
→ Go to Chapter 7 – Girded with Truth

☐ Righteousness (obedience vs compromise)
→ Go to Chapter 7 – Guarded by Righteousness

☐ Peace (stability vs agitation)
→ Go to Chapter 7 – Grounded in Peace

☐ Faith (trust vs fear)
→ Go to Chapter 7 – Shield of Faith

☐ Assurance (confidence vs accusation)
→ Go to Chapter 7 – Helmet of Salvation

☐ Word of God (readiness vs dullness)
→ Go to Chapter 7 – Sword of the Spirit

Am I thinking clearly or drifting under pressure?

☐ I am thinking clearly and truthfully.
☐ My thoughts are being pulled toward fear, lies, or extremes.
☐ I am rehearsing truth, not replaying the attack.
☐ I am focusing on obedience, not outcomes.

If my thinking feels unstable
→ Go to Chapter 8 – Guarding the Mindset

Am I remaining spiritually connected right now?

☐ I am staying near to the Lord.
☐ I am resisting isolation or withdrawal.
☐ I am maintaining prayer and the Word, even if it feels difficult.
☐ I am relying on God's strength, not my own.

If I feel distant or disconnected
→ Go to Chapter 9 – Strengthening the Spirit

Am I remaining faithful to my mission?

☐ I am remaining faithful to what God has called me to do.
☐ I am not withdrawing from responsibility or service.
☐ I am choosing obedience even when it feels costly.
☐ I am continuing forward, not quitting.

If I feel tempted to stop or step back
→ Go to Chapter 10 – Staying on Mission

Final Charge

You will face spiritual opposition again. Scripture is clear about that. The enemy does not stop because you finished a book, and victory is not measured by the absence of conflict. It is measured by faithfulness.

Do not be surprised when pressure returns. Do not panic when the fight feels familiar. You have been trained to recognize the attack, respond biblically, and stand where God has placed you. Use what you have learned. Return to the truth. Submit yourself to God. Resist the enemy. Hold your ground.

Remember this: you are not called to win battles in your own strength. You are called to stand in Christ. He has already secured the victory. Your responsibility is obedience—day by day, step by step, even when the battle is quiet and unseen.

So go forward steady, not fearful. Alert, not anxious. Faithful, not fatigued. When the pressure rises, stand. When the fight lingers, stand. And when the enemy presses hardest, stand still and trust the Lord who fights for you.

About the Author

Pastor Steven Pratt, Jr. is a missionary church planter and the founding pastor of *FaithWay Bible Baptist Church* in Calgary, Alberta.

Sent out with a burden to reach Canada with the gospel and establish strong, Bible-believing churches, he and his family launched *FaithWay* from a small gathering in their garage. Through seasons of growth, pressure, and spiritual opposition, the church has developed into a thriving, multi-ethnic congregation reaching communities across southern Calgary.

He is also the founder of *CanadaChurchPlanting.com*, a ministry dedicated to equipping and encouraging missionaries, church planters, and local churches across Canada.

Pastor Steven's preaching and writing are rooted in expository Scripture teaching and shaped by pastoral ministry on the front lines. His approach to spiritual warfare emphasizes biblical clarity, obedience, and dependence on Christ rather than fear, speculation, or sensationalism.

Pastor Steven, his wife Laura, and their daughter Elizabeth are missionaries sent out of *Bible Baptist Church* in Wilmington, Ohio. Together, they count it a privilege to serve the Lord in full-time ministry.

www.ingramcontent.com/pod-product-compliance
Lightning Source LLC
Chambersburg PA
CBHW032222080426
42735CB00008B/673